**Overcoming Common Problems**

# WHY BE AFRAID?

## How to overcome your fears

Dr Paul Hauck

## SHELDON PRESS
### LONDON

First published in the USA in 1975 by
The Westminster Press, Philadelphia, Pennsylvania

First published in Great Britain in 1981 by
Sheldon Press, SPCK, Marylebone Road, London NW1 4DU

Second impression 1984

Typeset by Computacomp (UK) Ltd,
Fort William, Scotland
Printed in Great Britain by
Biddles Ltd, Guildford, Surrey


ISBN 0 85969 337 6

# Contents

*This one is for my fearful clients—*
*who taught me a great deal about courage*

# Preface

This book is another in a series about emotional problems. It follows *Depression* and *Calm Down*. Previously I pointed out that depression is one of the most painful neurotic reactions, and anger is possibly the most common. Now we come to fear, which I think is one of the most chronic neurotic emotions. It has a way of clinging to a person so persistently that its effect is felt for much longer periods than depression or anger. An individual can become depressed, but sooner or later this mood will leave and be replaced by a neutral feeling or even a feeling of exhilaration. Anger can flare up quickly, but soon dies down. One can of course be angry or depressed for a lifetime, but even when that is the case, the person is not experiencing these feelings all the time. A fear of doing badly, however, can influence practically everything a person does each day of his life. It may not hurt as much as depression, or flare up as frequently as anger, but it will be there constantly, ready to disturb, year in and year out.

Another feature of fear is that it has a unique power to prevent one from fulfilling any potential. On its own it can destroy a man of genius and suppress any talents he might have. Depression can hold back ordinary men or women from doing what they are capable of only as long as the depression is relatively severe. But sooner or later they are able to get back to the business of living even though they are depressed. The same may be said for anger. In the midst of a feeling of fury we accomplish very little that is beneficial to ourselves or to others. However, even if we have lingering resentments or strong feelings of bitterness, we are still able to go about our jobs, drive our cars, balance our accounts, and so on.

Fear, however, is one of these emotions which can stifle talent no matter how great it is, even to the point where that talent becomes practically nonexistent. The singer who suffers from stage fright could have the voice of a Caruso, but it will never be heard by the world if he is afraid to perform. The student who has the intellect of an Isaac Newton may never attend a university because of fear of failure and humiliation.

In short, fear can be devastating in a special way that anger and depression cannot. Worse, it is a common emotion. Since all of us are afflicted by fear, anxiety, phobia, nervousness, or worry many times during our lives, and since these emotions reduce our potential as fulfilled human beings, I urge you to read the following pages with care and appreciation. In the pages that follow, you will find a full explanation of what causes our fears and what we can do about overcoming them. This is a practical book for anyone who thinks he can benefit through reading. Some will benefit enormously, while others will only profit minimally; either way you will gain an understanding of what causes nervousness, shyness, and other forms of fear. If you then want counselling, you will be that much better prepared to profit from it. Be bold, be daring, and read on.

# I

# A Glance at Our Most Common Fears

The fears and worries that threaten most lives are not the spectacular ones. Walking a tightrope over the Niagara Falls or putting your head into a lion's mouth are dangerous undertakings, but most of us are not likely to be exposed to these perils. The really frightening situations in life usually involve people, not animals or natural hazards, and the most frightening situations aren't usually dangerous. Yet we often behave towards one another and towards everyday events with such dread that we miss out on an enormous amount of pleasure throughout our lives. Let us look at several examples of normal fears from clients whom I have counselled and see if we can understand their problems.

## Fear of socializing

One of the most common fears people have is the fear of socializing. Men and women who can face wild animals and can do all kinds of dangerous things simply melt when it comes to going into a room full of strangers and making small talk. This harmless act terrifies them because they think that being rejected hurts. If you think this way too, then you're in for all kinds of pain, because your life is going to be empty.

Jim was such a person. He was divorced and was having a hard time finding new female friends to socialize with. He became so desperate that he attempted suicide several times. Finally he sought counselling to help him understand why he was not more successful at making friends.

Apparently when he was about twelve years old he was laughed at while dancing at a school function. Ever since then he has been afraid to get on the dance floor, except on a few occasions when he had several drinks under his belt. Even then he would ask his partner if he was acting too stiffly, or alternatively would insist that he didn't dance well and ask if she agreed.

His fear of being rejected was so intense that he only approached girls whom he regarded as ugly. He reasoned that if he asked only unattractive females, he could hardly be turned down since they didn't have much of a choice anyway and might be happy to receive his attention.

It did not dawn on Jim that his reason for failure at the socializing game was simply that he thought of himself as an undesirable person with whom nobody would want to be seen. As long as he held this negative view of himself it was hard for others to see him any other way.

If you give others the impression that you are not worth talking to, they sense your discomfort and tend to leave you alone. This is exactly the opposite of what you need and want. If people were more considerate, they would recognize your insecurity and make a point of talking to you or would seek you out rather than make you do the work. However, this is not the way human nature is. People do not come to the rescue of the outcast; they let such a person sit all night long in silent misery. People do not invite the shy person out of his home. Rather, they let him live out his life in loneliness if he is too afraid to overcome it.

Socializing successfully is never merely a matter of being good-looking or intelligent or having money. All of us have seen persons who are not especially attractive, not particularly bright, or not comfortable financially, who still enjoy a large circle of friends. This is only possible for persons who have a sense of self-esteem, who do not care too much whether they are loved, and who are willing to make the overture time and again. They do not fear initial rejection, knowing that sooner or later if they keep plugging away at asking people out or inviting them in someone is going to accept them.

Just as Jim would only seek out unattractive girls to assure himself of at least some success, Betty avoided any man who was aggressive, because she was afraid she couldn't handle him on a date. She had been scared of being pregnant ever since she was sixteen, and as a result went out mainly with passive men whom she couldn't stand. On the few occasions when she misjudged a date and found that he was a more self-assured fellow than she thought, she would spoil the date early in the evening so as to cool off any interest he might have in her.

Which hurt more? Was she hurt more because she might have been pressured by the man, or was she hurt more because she had spoiled the evening for herself and ended a potentially fine relationship? Fear usually involves two kinds of pain. One pain comes from doing what you are afraid of; the other pain comes from avoiding what you are afraid of. Either way, you are going to be uncomfortable. You cannot escape that. However, the pain connected with *doing* an activity is generally less in the long run than the pain connected with *avoiding* an activity. Had Betty recognized this, she would simply have gone out with more fellows who were aggressive so that she could have learned how to handle them, rather than spend her life running away from them. You cannot learn a task or skill unless you practise it. When she went out with passive men she was simply avoiding a problem, not learning how to live and deal with one.

All the while this was going on, Betty very much envied the great success her friend Judy was having with her boyfriends. Judy was the aggressive type who could turn a fellow on or off and didn't mind doing so. She had fun and was pursued by a number of men because the word got around that she was a pretty lively type, not cold, but cautious and sensible. Betty knew exactly what she had to do to get the same kind of success that Judy had, but she wouldn't do it. The end result was that Betty found herself quite lonely listening to Judy's exploits while she herself had nothing to report.

No matter how difficult it might sound just now, it *is* possible for you to change your fears of socializing and to overcome your shyness. One of the things you will want to do is change some of your traditional conceptions of what is proper behaviour, especially if you are a woman. More aggressive behaviour may be necessary if you are ever to overcome your shyness. Being more socially alive is also going to take nerve and aggressiveness that you may never have exercised in your whole life up to now.

Pat, a widowed woman in her forties, was in dire need of a more interesting social life but either did not know how to pursue it or was afraid to do what was necessary. I instructed her to read Albert Ellis' *The Intelligent Woman's Guide to Manhunting*. When I next saw her I learned that she had been so busy with her social life that she had to work out a way of cooling it down.

"I got the courage to go on a blind date for the first time in my life and that opened the door. I had three new dates shortly after that." Once, when meeting one of her old boyfriends at a restaurant, she went up to him and asked, "Where is your wife?" When he told her that he was divorced, her immediate answer was, "Why not ring me sometime?" This kind of straightforwardness and aggression would have been totally unthinkable for her before she saw how necessary it was to become more assertive. This may not be a role you will enjoy, but if you want results, this is what it takes.

## Fear of ridicule

This is a particularly disturbing bugbear to a lot of people. It keeps them from fulfilling themselves and being as happy as they easily could be. Toni was a thick-set girl who tended to stay at home a great deal because she was afraid of being ridiculed about her weight. She had a very pretty face and just enough weight that some men would have considered her well-rounded and pleasingly plump. However, she hated those extra pounds and would not accept any of the many invitations she received.

I advised her to go out even though she was heavier than she liked, because then she might feel better. This in turn might give her the motivation to diet, because it would pull her out of her depression. However, she had such a disappointing time of it when she did go out (because her thoughts were always on her weight) that she simply gave it up and decided not to do any dating or socializing until she did lose a few pounds.

So there she was, stuck on her own mental merry-go-round. She didn't lose weight so she got depressed and didn't go out. Had she made enough dates, she might not have minded the extra weight—or she might have felt so good eventually that she would have found the energy to do the dieting.

She thought that by avoiding ridicule she was saving herself a lot of pain. But this again was not true. By avoiding the fear, she simply replaced the unpleasantness of ridicule with the unpleasantness of being lonely. Which would have been easier to tolerate, being alone or being ridiculed? I maintain that this girl would not have been ridiculed in the first place. But even if she had been, it would have been much easier for her to tolerate some comments about her weight and to learn to laugh them off than to be miserable day in and day out for months on end while she lived a lonely life at home.

Simply avoiding fearsome situations does not remove discomfort. You are going to be frustrated one way or the other; there is discomfort in changing and there is discomfort in not changing. However, the discomfort connected with changing your behaviour or with overcoming your fears has an ending, whereas the annoyance that you have if you don't face your fears can go on until you die.

### The two most common fears

If you were asked what most people are afraid of, what would you say? Would it be one of the following: aircraft, dying, disease, unemployment, war, physical punishment? I would think so. However, from my observations and those of a great number of other psychotherapists, it is clear that these are not the greatest fears people have. The two most common fears are the fear of rejection and the fear of failure. These two fears are possessed by millions of people at least some of the time, and a good many people have them almost all of the time. The fear of rejection is probably more prevalent than the fear of failure but the two are close. People are often afraid to fail for the very reason that they might be rejected if they do.

It was the fear of being rejected that made Jim tremble every time he tried to propose to his fiancée. Whenever he was about to pop the question he would get nervous and so afraid of being turned down that he would keep the question to himself and go home with all his lovely speeches unspoken. Apparently they were exceptional speeches. He had months in which to make up fantastically romantic statements to his girlfriend and to make that moment of proposal a memorable one. Instead, when he finally got nerve enough to do it after months of waiting he lost his cool and simply blurted out, "Well, are we going to get married or aren't we?"

Then there was Louise. She went through the sort of thing that can happen when you are afraid of hurting someone's feelings. Pat, her older girlfriend, was often kind enough to babysit for her. Louise used Pat so constantly to sit with her three-year-old son that before she knew it Pat had taken over the role of a mother in a most frightening way. When Louise wanted her child to wear a certain coat, or to play with certain children, Pat would object strongly, and she frequently had her way until Louise began to see what was happening. She then stood up for herself even though it would cost her the friendship. But this was not accomplished until Pat had actually suggested that Louise allow her to adopt the child. It was at this point that the mother simply did not care how hurt her friend might be. She stood up to her and forbade her to babysit any longer and simply ended the friendship. But it was fear of hurting this woman in the first place which allowed the whole matter to get so drastically out of hand.

The fear of rejection and the fear of failure were combined in a most unique way in the case of Rose, who was laughed at sarcastically once during love-making with her husband. After that she turned very cold towards him and simply could not

6

perform spontaneously. The marriage eventually ended in divorce, but her fear of rejection and failure hung on with such tenacity that she could not relax even in the company of other men, for fear they too might laugh if she allowed herself to become intimate and romantic. It baffled her that she was so cold, since she wanted very much to permit herself to get close to some of the men she knew. However, it was not until she recalled the incident of being laughed at by her husband that she realized how hurt she had been and how she had let that foolish behaviour on his part upset her for a period of about ten years. Once she understood, fear subsided.

Fear of rejection can be so powerful that some people will do practically anything to avoid it, including the surrender of all their self-respect. Sue was such a woman. She married a much older man early in life and had three children by him. Although she brought him coffee in bed, and took on two jobs to help support him, he still left her. It affected her whole life. She could not stand up to her own father for fear that he would reject her, despite the fact that he completely ignored her and did favours for Sue's husband. For example, it was all right for Sue's husband to visit her father, but she couldn't visit him. In the end she had neither a husband nor a father who would talk to her, and her own three children simply brushed her aside as insignificant. All this happened simply because she thought that to have the love and affection of these people she had to do anything they asked of her. Yet, as so frequently happens in such cases, the more you do for people who are unreasonably demanding, the more impossible they become, and the less they love you in the long run.

Bill was one of those fellows who greets you with a handshake like a vice, a salesman's smile, and a ready line of chatter as though he were the life of the party. All this behaviour had only one motivation: to avoid being rejected. Bill was playing the stereotype of the popular, well-accomplished boy, and he was making such a bad job of it that even all of his so-called charm simply did not work. There was something unreal about it and everyone except Bill knew it.

In all the above examples the problems were created because the person felt compelled to do what he thought was expected. Otherwise, it seemed, he would be rejected by those persons whose love he thought he had to have. This business of having to be perfect and having to be loved by others is sheer nonsense. That is not to say that being loved or that doing well at whatever we attempt is not important; it *is* important, indeed it may be among the most vital things that we do. The point the fearful person fails to realize, however, is that being perfect and being loved all the time are not essential. These are desirable objects but *hardly necessary* for one's well-being or sense of self-esteem. We can be rejected by others and still not reject ourselves. It is when *we* reject *ourselves* that we get into emotional trouble, not when others reject us. This is where so many neurotics fail to correct their problems. They think, as some persons in the above examples thought, that if they could finally get that certain person in their lives to love them, they themselves were bound to be fine people. But this is not so. Having others love you proves nothing about you; it only proves something about their tastes. If you want to get over the fear of rejection and failure, learn to accept yourself if others reject you and even if you fail. Then, no matter what happens, you won't be down in the mouth, and self-hating. With this strength, try to figure out why you were rejected or why you made the mistake, and then try to correct it. In this fashion you can improve your performance each time, and you can figure out what it takes to get the approval of certain people. But even if you never get their approval it still will not be so depressing, because you will have realized that being loved by others is not of the utmost importance.

Then what is important in this life? The truly important thing is not to be hated by others. When someone hates you that's truly serious, because he may shoot you or make your life a misery. But not being loved is not going to kill you. Therefore I think we should be much more concerned about who our

8

enemies are than whether someone whom we like very much happens to like us just as much.

In the following pages a number of practical steps will be given to help fight these two very common problems. Work on these very hard, because if you learn to overcome the fear of failure and rejection, then practically all you have left to overcome is your fear of wildebeests attacking you, the polar caps melting, or Halley's comet landing in your back garden.

# 2

# The Psychology of Fear

I know of no set of terms in psychological literature that are as confusing as the following five: fear, anxiety, phobia, worry, and nervousness. It is truly amazing that we confuse these terms in our professional writings and speeches as often as we do. Therefore, before we go any further, we need to have a clear understanding of how these various terms differ from each other.

## Fear

When you are afraid of something and you consciously know what it is that you are afraid of, that is a fear. For example, if you were told this afternoon that business is slowing down and you may be laid off, you'd naturally become uneasy about the possibility of losing your job. You would have *a fear*, because you'd *know* what it is you are afraid of. The same would be true if a robber entered your house and pointed a gun at you. You would probably be afraid of what he might do. You would have a fear, because you'd known what it is that scares you. You can be afraid of death, high places, elevators, and so on. You may even be afraid of becoming afraid. If you know what it is that you are afraid of, we say you are experiencing a fear (or various fears).

## Anxiety

When you do not know what you are afraid of, you are experiencing anxiety. Suppose that one afternoon you are told that business in your shop is slow and that some workers will be laid off. Later in the day you become tense. But you are not aware that it is the news you received earlier which has made you tense. We would call that feeling anxiety.

Anxiety can work like fear in that one can be anxious over

literally anything, even anxiety itself. But always remember that anxiety is an unconscious state, never a conscious one. This is not always agreed upon in psychological literature, and I am here taking some liberties by choosing to define anxiety in my own terms. However, because there has been so much confusion on the issue in the past, I feel that some order is called for. I am therefore choosing to define a fear specifically and *only* as a feeling of threat from a cause of which you are aware, and anxiety as a feeling of threat from a cause of which you are not aware.

## Phobia

A phobia is a combination of fear and anxiety. It occurs when you do not know what it is that you are afraid of *but you think you know*. Furthermore, the object that you think you fear must symbolically represent the actual fear you have.

Suppose you are afraid of using lifts. This can be a fear and it can also be a phobia. If it is truly the lift that you are afraid of, then we would say you have a fear of lifts. But if you are afraid of falling in social status and you do not want to recognize this fear, then you might unconsciously express this fear as a fear of falling down a lift shaft. You have converted your fear of falling socially into a fear of falling in a lift shaft and presumably you have solved your problem, since all you have to do now to avoid your fear of being rejected socially is not to get into lifts.

I recall the case of a very nervous young woman who came to me because she was terrified that she might discover a snake or a lizard whenever she moved into a new home. Even when she went to bed every night she would have to shake the sheets out thoroughly to make sure that there was not some kind of reptile lying there between the sheets. This got so bad that even if she saw a centipede scurrying across her kitchen floor or a worm outside on the drive, she would go into a panic. Sometimes it took a great deal of effort on the part of her husband to calm her down and to convince her that she did not have to pack up all her things and go and find another flat.

I treated this condition for a number of weeks as though it were a fear. That is, I presumed that it was actually snakes, lizards, centipedes, and worms that she was afraid of. I encouraged her to study these insects from a biological point of view and referred her to the encyclopedia to look at pictures of them and know more about them. I further instructed her to go to the biology department of the university and to study these creatures at close range. For a while it appeared as though she was becoming so familiar with them that she could disregard them. I was going on the theory that if one is afraid of something, then becoming very familiar with it removes the fear. But this was not the case with this girl.

It then finally occurred to me that perhaps we were not dealing with fear at all but with a phobia instead. This meant that the snake or lizard would have to represent *something else* she was terrified of, and that it was this other thing that I had to look for and get her to understand. When I explored her past, it turned out that she had been molested by her cousin, who would sometimes sleep over at her house when they were children and would sneak into her room at night and forcibly fondle her.

She naturally felt very guilty about this, but because her parents were quick to judge she did not dare entrust them with this information. She felt certain that they would accuse her of having seduced this boy. This guilty knowledge she kept to herself all those years. After she was married, her sexual activities reawakened her sense of guilt, and she translated that guilt onto these insects in symbolic form. It was only when she could talk about the shame and guilt she had always hidden from herself concerning these childhood activities that she overcame her fear, and at that point her phobia lifted. She was then able to go to bed without checking the sheets and only gave a worm on the drive a second glance.

It is important to make this distinction because the literature suggests that anybody who has a strange or irrational fear really has a phobia. This is nonsensical, for who is to say what is a strange fear? There are people who are afraid of lifts because they know something about mechanics and they realize there can be malfunctions and that all lifts can fall. That does not have to be a phobia. A person can be afraid of lifts simply because they can be dangerous. Similarly, you can be afraid of high places simply because you can fall from them and be injured. That is a fear. But you could be afraid of high places because they symbolize success and you are a person afraid to succeed. That is a phobia. If I am afraid of flying saucers—and I would consider this a very strange fear for me—this would not necessarily be a phobia, no matter how odd it appeared to others. If flying saucers do not represent anything to me other than flying saucers, I would have a fear. But if I were afraid of flying saucers because they symbolically represented my Aunt Tillie, who once scalded me when her cup and saucer slipped out of her hand, then I would have a phobia.

## Worry and nervousness

Worry and nervousness are particular kinds of fear in that they seldom ease over long periods. The person knows what he is afraid of but he just can't let the matter rest. I, for example, am probably afraid of piranha fish, the kind that can quickly eat a whole man, but I don't worry about them all the time. The worrier, however, focuses upon the feared object and can't let that fear out of his thoughts. He dwells upon it, thinks about it all the time, and in short, worries himself sick over it.

All five conditions we have described are varieties of fear. Three are conscious (fear, nervousness, and worry), two are unconscious (anxiety and phobia), and one is also symbolic (phobia).

# 3

# The Real Cause of Fear

Millions of people believe that they become afraid because they find themselves in some dangerous situation. They would say, for example, that being on an aircraft *makes* them afraid. They would further say that being told by a physician that they have cancer and will die within three months also *has* to make them afraid. Being in a war, being held up on the street, being rejected, doing badly on an important task—these are all thought to be the causes of fear, nervousness, worry, or anxiety.

Until recently psychologists agreed that fear was caused directly by the things that happened to us. Now, however, we have come to see that this is not the complete process in the development of fear. Another step is very directly involved, and that is *the way we think* about these events and respond to them.

Let's suppose a worker named Tom is approached by his boss one morning and told: "Tom, you've been late several times this month. Watch out." This comment could cause any number of psychological reactions in Tom, all of which would have been created completely by him, not by what his boss said or what he might do. If Tom were to become upset over this remark, he would do it in somewhat the following way.

First, he would have to make a mountain out of a molehill and tell himself that this remark by his boss was *terrible*, *awful*, and *dreadfully* serious. In other words, he would have to make a *catastrophe* out of what the boss said and out of what might happen as a result of his boss's attitude. We call this *catastrophizing*. To do this Tom would have to think such thoughts as, "Oh dear, it looks like I'm in trouble, and *that's awful*." Or he might say, "I think I am going to lose my job, and *that would be the end of the world*." Or he might even

14

think, "My boss is rejecting me, and *I can't stand it*."

Notice, in the three examples above, that there are two statements being made in each of the quotations. We can completely agree with the first half of each of these statements, namely Tom might certainly be in trouble, he might lose his job, and his boss might reject him. However, we cannot in any way agree (*a*) that it is awful if he is in trouble or (*b*) that it would be the end of the world if he lost his job or (*c*) that he could not stand it if his boss rejected him. Tom himself believes that, however. Therefore he goes on thinking that he is facing something so dangerous and so shattering that it is no longer just a *sad* thing that is happening to him, but a truly *tragic* thing. Once he convinces himself that he is facing a life-and-death issue, he is automatically disturbed.

The kind of disturbance he will have after he catastrophizes to himself will depend upon a few other things that he says to himself at this point. If he has one set of thoughts, he will become depressed. If he goes along another track, he will become angry. And if he has a third set of thoughts, he will become nervous, worried, fearful, or anxious.

For example, Tom might say: "There I go again, always messing it up and making people hate me. I deserve to be fired from this job. I'm no good." In this case we would expect him to become depressed because of his guilt and self-blame.

On the other hand, Tom might say: "What does he think he is getting at criticizing me for being a few minutes late? I work twice as hard as anyone else around here, so he shouldn't complain at me and threaten to fire me. Who does he think he is?" We can be sure that Tom would become quite angry after he worked himself into this mood.

But suppose Tom were to say: "Oh, this is dreadful, I can't stand it. I'm going to lose my job and that will be the end of the world, and, because this is really on the cards now, I must think it through all today and tomorrow and worry over it at all times." We can be certain that Tom will develop a worried or nervous condition at the very least.

The interesting and fascinating point which I am attempting to make is that emotional disturbances come only from the way we talk to ourselves about our problems, not from the problems themselves. We are never made depressed, angry, or fearful by the things that happen to us, only by the way we think to ourselves about them. This means that no one has ever angered you, depressed you, or made you nervous in your whole life once you grew past the age of childhood. Children do not have the capacity to think clearly and logically and, therefore, they are at the mercy of the adults who can directly upset them with their talk and actions. However, as adolescents or adults we have the capacity to understand people's remarks as the harmless things which they are. Whenever we are upset during adolescence or adulthood, it is always we who are upsetting ourselves; the events themselves are not responsible.

This analysis describes the ABC theory of emotions proposed by Albert Ellis, Ph.D., the founder of rational-emotive psychotherapy. A stands for the events that happen to us every day. B stands for what we tell ourselves about these everyday events—for example: "It is terrible when my boss talks harshly to me." C stands for the consequences, not from A, but from B, representing the emotions we experience because of what we have told ourselves at point B, not because of what has happened to us at point A.

Therefore, if you want to undo any nervous reaction or any emotional problem, you can achieve this in one of two ways. You can go back to A and remove the frustration; you can divorce an impossible wife, change from an impossible job, or find money if you are poor. Or, in the event that you can't change anything at point A, you can change the way you think about your problem at point B. Then you might say to yourself: "I *can* stand to be married to this person even though I don't love her any longer. I don't want to stay with this job, but it is the only one I can get so I will just have to *lump* it. And I haven't found any money on the streets, so I will remain poor. And that isn't going to kill me even though I don't

16

particularly like this kind of living." In short, it is our challenging the beliefs we have about things which happen to us that puts our minds at rest.

This is the beauty of the rational-emotive approach to psychology. It states quite clearly (and there is a great deal of clinical evidence to support the claim) that you can be unafraid even though you are in dangerous situations. But to do this, of course, you will have to learn how to challenge and question those neurotic notions which have upset you so often in the past. You will have to learn how to come up with those sensible and healthy ideas which you will want to use to replace these neurotic notions. In every case where you are nervous you can assume that you have automatically told yourself (a) that something is a catastrophe and (b) that, if it is a catastrphe, you *must* worry and fret and focus upon it at all times. If you never did either of these, you could never be afraid of anything. The rest of this book will attempt to show you how you can stop catastrophizing. You will be taught to challenge the idea that you must worry over something unpleasant just because it might happen to you.

### Being afraid of fear

It is obvious that one can be afraid of anything. What is generally not appreciated is that you can be as afraid of *becoming* afraid as of having a bomb blow you up. Being afraid of becoming afraid is a great deal more common than some of the fears of physical dangers are. Once a person starts to become afraid that he will become upset and experience more fear, he is going to do just that: experience more fear.

Suppose you notice one day that your breathing is not quite what it usually is. You wonder if there is something wrong with your lungs, so you begin to breathe faster in order to make your breathing more normal. Suppose, however, that this makes you somewhat light-headed and causes a pain in the chest, which alarms you. At this point you begin to become afraid of what is happening to you. You try even harder to make your breathing normal. The longer you do this the more irregular and unnatural your breathing becomes. Soon you are breathing in such an inefficient manner that you really have trouble getting enough air. At that point you become noticeably upset because you have something truly to be concerned about. The longer this keeps up the more you find it impossible to keep your mind off your breathing, until it becomes difficult to breathe normally. That's the type of thing that generally happens to people when they focus on something so hard that the whole operation loses it spontaneity.

Generally speaking, the more you worry about something, the worse it gets. Many of the bodily functions we worry about would operate fairly normally on their own if we simply didn't pay as much attention to them.

Sex is a particularly good case in point. A man who may not be able to perform very well one night may begin to wonder and worry so much about what happened to him that he might think about that problem all night long and the next day. Now his mind is no longer on sex but on the possibility of his failing his partner again. When he then attempts to make love again he may find that he is not thinking about her at all but about how she might laugh at him or how embarrassing it would be if he could not perform normally. And because his mind is really not on sex but on his possible humiliation, he fails to perform adequately. If this is what happens the second night, he is probably more fearful that it will happen the third. Then, because he is more afraid of that, it does happen a third time. And it will eventually happen a fourth and a fifth time. Constantly dwelling upon the possibility of failing becomes the reason that he fails.

This tendency to make mountains out of molehills is the first step in being afraid of fear. A young lady I once counselled began postgraduate work some years after having achieved a very fine record as an undergraduate student. However, because she had not been in college for a number of years she found the first two months very difficult and demanding. She then began to wonder whether she could manage the studies at all and began to panic, thinking that she might have to drop out. At this point she had only a fear of failing in college. The longer this went on, the more she became afraid not just of failing in her work but also of becoming nervous again. The fear of becoming nervous began to bother her even more than the fear of failing. By the time she saw me she was more fearful of losing control of herself than of not doing the graduate work. This is frequently the direction which fear takes. People start out by being afraid of one event and in the process of being afraid they notice that the feeling of fear itself is quite unpleasant. Then they stop being afraid of the initial thing and become afraid of becoming afraid. They then worry about worrying or become anxious over becoming anxious. The ultimate fear in this cycle is that they are afraid they will lose their self-control and have a breakdown.

A sweet old lady I worked with once was so certain she was going to go insane that she had the habit of putting her kitchen knives away in the drawers whenever she had finished using them. This habit had gone on for a period of twenty years. She was initially afraid years ago that she might die during childbirth. Her child was delivered well enough and it was a healthy baby, but she did not forget the fear of dying she had experienced. She was afraid that this fear might return, and because she kept thinking about it she became anxious, but didn't know what it was she feared. I explained to her that she was afraid of becoming tense and that if she would no longer worry about being tense, she might calm down.

"But how am I supposed to calm down, doctor? This is a terrible feeling that comes over me. I can't stand the thought of going through another anxious spell."

"But why can't you? You've been having this thing for twenty years and you still haven't lost your mind. Why should the next time drive you insane?"

"Well, it could happen sometime, couldn't it?"

"Hardly. You say you have had one to three of these

episodes every day for the last twenty years. If we reckon it conservatively at one nervous spell per day for twenty years, that comes to a total of 7,300 anxiety episodes. Now if you haven't gone beserk and butchered your family with those knives after 7,300 times, why do you suppose you would do it the next time? I certainly can't accept the idea that you're really a vicious and dangerous person. Instead, I think the only thing that will happen when you have your next fear reaction will be that you will simply get nervous and shake and *that will be all*. Never in those twenty years time has it ever gone beyond the point where you simply were very tense. What makes you think that it will be different this next time?"

"But doesn't this kind of thing eventually lead to going crazy?" she asked with trembling lips.

"No. Being afraid and being psychotic are two separate things entirely. We find no evidence that people who have repeated anxiety attacks such as you have had eventually lose their minds. On the contrary, they simply remain pretty normal neurotic people."

"Then you're suggesting, doctor, that if I just don't pay any attention to this, I won't have it?"

"Yes, but it's not quite that easy. What I am suggesting is that if you don't make so much of it, the anxiety spells will begin to get shorter and less frequent rather than worse. Then eventually you will find that you won't have any at all. That's got to make sense, doesn't it? After all, if you don't worry about something, how can you get worried?"

This woman gratefully did see the point and was able to make less and less of her episodes of tension until she could truly tell herself that this uncomfortable feeling which was coming over her was only number 7,301, and if she didn't make a big fuss over the whole thing it would just disappear.

The clue to handling fear reactions is simply not to handle them at all. The harder you fight these things the worse they get. It makes absolutely no difference what the fear happens to be, there is no reason why we have to lose our heads over it. In the final analysis the anxiety for that episode is going to last just so long and then it will stop, just as it has stopped thousands of times before. Therefore, the next time you have one of these anxiety spells, look at your watch and see what time it is. Then try to ignore the whole thing as much as possible and see how long it takes to regain your calm. The next time it happens, check the time again and say to yourself: "O.K., this is nothing to get panicky over. I am simply having an anxiety attack and in all likelihood it will only last $x$ number of minutes, just as it did yesterday. If I don't do any catastrophizing over the fact that I am about to become very tense, I will eventually become less and less tense."

## Fear of death

It is commonly assumed by many people that death is at least one of those things we have to be afraid of. But I contend that the fear of death is no different from any other fear. The things we fear are usually very unpleasant, and death does not strike me as being any more unpleasant than many other dangers.

I shall never forget the time a pleasant and intelligent woman came to me insisting that her horoscope indicated that on a certain day she would die. This was supposed to justify her feelings of tension. But I insisted that as far as I could see she had no justification for being nervous and jittery. I then pointed out that she had taken her life into her hands when she got into the car to drive to my office. She was certainly endangered every time she drove, but it never occurred to her to feel panicky over that possibility. Her bedroom was located over the boiler and it never occurred to her that she was in some danger that the boiler might blow up. The possibility of choking to death in a restaurant on a chicken bone never seriously preyed on her mind either. In short, she was constantly under the threat of death but never let it bother her.

## Unconscious fears

The type of fears I have been referring to are conscious ones that have a degree of common sense to them. Another category of fears, however, are the unconscious ones. These are no different from other fears, except that they are tied to some incidents from childhood that we have forgotten. Dealing with an unconscious fear requires corrective measures that are not called for when dealing with conscious fears. It is usually necessary to go back into the past to discover the elements that created the fear in the first place. Then a person is better prepared to understand why he is currently so fearful. Take the case of Ms. Baker. When she was about six years old her sister took apart one of her dolls and dangled it before her. For some strange reason she became terrified at what she saw. Now, as a young adult, she is still very upset if she sees dolls with parts missing. She becomes tearful and has nightmares of dolls with their heads off or their feet off and their parts lying around on her bed.

To overcome this fear she even attempted to dismantle dolls by herself. She would take off their heads but could really go no further than this. Sometimes when she comes upon a doll with its head off or its legs off she becomes so terrified that she screams.

How can we understand this condition? Obviously some strange set of events took place in her childhood which would have to be exposed first before she could get any control over the present fear. Furthermore it is quite probable that the fear of a dismantled doll is in this case actually a phobia. We can hardly imagine her literally being afraid of dismantled dolls, but we might imagine her being afraid of babies being pulled apart or of persons who might harm children. These would be the clues to look for if she wanted to explore the possible dynamics of this problem. Simply because a fear has existed for years does not mean that it will be unconscious.

To show the difference between a conscious and a truly unconscious fear (such as Ms. Baker had), let us look at the case of Ms. Wood. During her childhood she was always beaten in competition by her older sister. Eventually both sisters married. They got along quite well with each other while both of their husbands were alive. However, the older girl's husband died, and it was at this point that Ms. Wood became fearful that her sister would now begin to win Mr. Wood over to her affections. She had some evidence that something like this might happen because her sister occasionally needed a man's help around the house and Mr. Wood was called upon and willingly obliged. This revived the old fear in Ms. Wood that her sister would eventually snatch her husband away from her and be the winner again as she always had been in their childhood.

Notice now that this is not an unconscious fear, just a long-standing one. Ms. Wood was fully aware of what had happened in childhood and what was likely to happen now. She was not afraid of anything other than losing her husband to a very competitive sister. This is the way it had always been, and she had no reason to believe that she would not be the loser again in a match against her sister.

Some fears appear to be phobias when actually they are nothing but fears that have existed for a long time because the person has refused to face them. Mary, a young lady in her twenties, remembered being kissed by an old man in a bathroom when she was about two years old. She developed a fear of bathrooms after that and would never lock the bathroom door for fear that she might be locked in with someone. Nor would she be around old men or go into places where she might be accosted by one. It troubles her to go up dark staircases or to be alone in her apartment. She has a gun to protect her as well as two dogs. However, none of this protection is enough to settle her nerves. She still has a fear that older men are going to accost her.

One could see this as a fear symbolizing something entirely different from the fear of old men—e.g., a desire to give in to old men, or a fear that her strong attachment toward her father might be carried too far if she didn't fight it in this fashion (so she might be fighting an Oedipus complex out of guilt).

However, it is also possible that she was simply scared by an older man when she was a child and never got over it, just as some people are scared by dogs when they are children and never truly overcome that fear. In Mary's case it was suggested that she simply had a fear rather than a phobia and that she should be around older men more frequently to show herself that she really did have the capacity to shut them off if they began to get too bold with her. She was after all a strong and healthy young lady and could probably outrun them, or notify the police, or defend herself if needed. She had apparently taken the attitude that she was still a two-year-old child who was at the mercy of any older man who might make an advance towards her. Once she began to see that she was no longer a helpless child with respect to the possible advances of older men, she began to relax and could be around them with a feeling of confidence and lack of anxiety. This permitted her to be friendly with a number of them in the secure knowledge that she was in no great danger.

# 4

## Neurotic Characteristics of Fear

A neurotic, as Albert Ellis succinctly put it, is a non-stupid person who behaves stupidly. This means that if you are facing an unpleasant situation and you make yourself *more* upset, that is a stupid act. Therefore it is neurotic. I further suggest that it is neurotic to feel afraid of being attacked by a lion, shot by a firing squad, or bombed by an aircraft, and so on.

You may protest that this sounds ridiculous. Although I myself might be afraid of these very situations, I see no sense in getting *more* upset over some unpleasant event than necessary. If a lion is going to eat me, I certainly don't want to have a nervous breakdown before I die. Granted that it is extremely difficult not to became afraid, it nevertheless makes sense in principle. The difference between a neurotic reaction and a non-neurotic reaction depends upon *how much* I am concerned with what is happening. As long as I am concerned about my being injured by a lion I will try to hide under a desk, throw things at him, jump out of a window, or scream for help. If I did none of those things, I would be out of my mind and not a healthy person at all. Doing something about my problem would be a sign of common sense. But I hope I would be able to do something in a rather calm manner, even though the situation itself is desperate.

It is being *excessively* concerned that leads to neurotic behaviour. At that point not only would I scream and throw something at the lion but I would likely become completely rattled and hysterical and lose all sense of where to hide and might in fact injure myself. I would be dying a thousand times. I would be on the verge of an emotional breakdown when in fact I hadn't even been touched. This is the result of overconcern, not concern. In a serious situation I think it is sensible and proper to show concern, but never overconcern.

25

And how are we to know when the occasion demands one rather than the other? The answer is simple. When you are painfully upset, you are automatically overconcerned. When you are not painfully upset but are working on the problem, you are merely concerned.

For example: if you are afraid of losing your job, you had better be concerned about your boss's feelings towards you; you had better get to work on time and do a good job. If you are unconcerned about these things, you will likely lose your job, and that would be self-defeating. But feeling afraid of losing your job might also cause you to lose your job, because you would worry so much about whether you were doing everything correctly, or you might pester your boss for signs of approval so consistently, that he might get sick of you and finally fire you anyway. Therefore I firmly believe that neurotic fear is always bad and that calm concern is usually good.

## How we learn to be afraid

We are taught to be afraid. Someone, usually our parents, tells us when we are children that it is dangerous to get near a big dog, to touch a hot stove, and to pick up a knife by its blade. We soon learn to be afraid of those things because of the emotional scenes people make. If we get hurt in the process of disobeying, we soon learn to fear the objects we were warned against.

Many things we fear are perfectly harmless, but we have been taught to be afraid of them nevertheless. Girls are taught to be afraid of snakes, but boys are not. A girl screams when asked to touch a toad, but a boy puts it in his pocket. The only explanation for these two attitudes is the fact that one person has been taught to be afraid and the other has been taught to be unafraid. The fear has nothing to do with the object itself, only what we make of it.

Fear is taught in the same way that prejudice, love, or mathematics is taught. The point is made to you over and over until you accept it. Moreover, you watch others become upset and afraid under certain circumstances, and before you know it you unthinkingly accept their belief and follow suit. For example, a child who watches his mother scoot under the table when there is a thunderstorm is bound to develop a queasy feeling about severe weather. The mother and the son are repeating to themselves the same neurotic statement that always leads to fear, namely, that if something is dangerous or fearsome one should worry about it, become frightened over it, dwell upon it, and focus upon it constantly.

## Using fear to control others

The idea of using our own neurotic and disturbing emotions to control other people is not at all strange to our experience. Children scream and act violently in order to get others to give in to them. Adults have their own ways of seeking the same ends. Everyone does this and has seen others do it. However, what is not generally so widely appreciated is that many people will use fear in the same way to control others. In the case of fear, however, the people who are afraid expect the others around them to feel sorry for them because of what will make them suffer. They also expect others to make exceptions and excuses for them since they are so terrified. How can one expect a terrified person to be responsible under the circumstances?

Ms. Lufton was a particularly good case of a woman who was controlled by her husband's tensions. This man was discharged from the Army with a medical disability and he was being paid because he had a psychiatric disability. Naturally he was not eager to give up his periods of anxiety because it would also mean the loss of a pension. But more than this, by the time I saw the family he had persuaded his wife to believe in his incapacity so completely that she went out and worked while he stayed home and took care of the cooking and the children. He was a mason by trade and managed to do a significant amount of building in his garden. He had also built a wall at the front of the house. But to suggest that he should go out and make a

27

living being a mason simply filled his heart with dread. His wife saw how upset he was over this, so she never pushed it. As a result he remained at home living the life of a lord while his wife slaved away more and more.

To see how false this whole thing was, however, one needs only to know that when the wife became ill and incapacitated he was able to arouse himself very easily to take over all the responsibilities until she recovered. The moment she was able to resume her activities he began to show signs of nervousness until his wife was forced to take over again.

## We are not consistent in our fears

One of the most remarkable things about fears is that we are pretty choosy about what we are afraid of. Some of us are afraid of robbers attacking us at night but not afraid of jumping out of an aircraft. The classic example is that of Miles Standish, the American pioneer, who was not afraid of the rigours of the frontier, or fighting Indians, but was terrified of rejection by Priscilla Mullens.

Perhaps an even better illustration of just how inconsistent and selective we are about fears is the case of Shirley. She was in most respects a fairly stable person. However, she felt terrified of making car journeys during bad weather. She had seen a bad accident one night and was afraid to drive when it was dark from that time on.

This same woman, however, is a policewoman and has to deal with some rather dangerous characters. She has been shot at, swung at, and threatened, and has taken it all calmly. In one instance a young man threw her up against the wall and threatened her with a knife. She walked away from the entire incident completely undisturbed.

All of us are familiar with examples of inconsistency about fears. The joke about the female bullfighter who was frightened by a mouse is not as strange as it might first appear. This example and others like it can easily serve to demonstrate just how we manipulate our fears and how it is not the things themselves which make us afraid, but rather how we regard them. It is difficult to recognize health and stability in ourselves when we are so inconsistent about which things we become afraid of.

## Fears tend to spread

One of the major reasons I think fear is unhealthy is that when you develop one fear you tend to develop two or more soon afterwards. And if nothing is done with these fears, they in turn tend to breed more fears, until a person can get to the point where he is practically paralyzed. I shall never forget the case of a woman who had a hand-washing obsession. She was terrified that she might pick up germs from touching the usual objects around her house. Instead of deliberately touching things in order to dispel her fear, she gave in to it and began to touch less and less. Finally she found herself in bed with her hands up in the air crying pitifully that she was doomed to stay there, since she could not move lest she touch something.

Another client that I can recall illustrates this tendency for fears to spread. She was afraid to touch things, but in her case it was her clothing after she had smoked a cigarette. If she went to her bedroom, opened the wardrobe door and then touched one of her dresses and it occurred to her that she had not first washed her hands to free them of the smoke from her last cigarette, she would then have to have that garment dry-cleaned. She would have to wash the handle of the wardrobe door with soap and water, and she would have to scrub the door to the bedroom and any part of the wall that she touched in the process of inspecting her garment.

Even on the way to my office in order to rid herself of these fears, she became quite upset over the possibility of coming to a traffic light and having it turn amber. At that moment she dreaded having to decide whether to go through the amber light or to stop. If she stopped, someone behind her might angrily honk his horn to urge her to go through. Or if she went through, she might find the light changing while she was half way across the junction. She made so much of this that at times it was difficult for her to leave the house and attend to her affairs in town.

## The fruits of fear

1    *Inferiority*. It is little recognised that fearful people tend to regard themselves as inferior. An inferiority complex goes hand in hand with being afraid of everyone. Therefore, if you allow yourself to be brow-beaten and ordered around by others, you are going to lose confidence in yourself and feel unable to stand up for your own rights. When you feel unworthy enough you will become afraid to face life on your own. You will need the support and direction of that stronger person who is always telling you what to do. This is particularly true of the woman who is intimidated by her man. She thinks her husband will yell at her and not make love to her, or that he will give her a bad time in some way, so she becomes meek and passive and lets her partner order her around most shamefully until she becomes meek as a mouse, and depressed, or until she becomes so fed up that she gets a divorce.

2    *Shyness*. Along with the feeling of inferiority another consequence of being afraid is shyness. Shy people are afraid of standing up for themselves, think that they are not as good as others, and are afraid of being rejected to such a degree that they can't even look other people in the eye. One young fellow I once counselled was treated so badly at home, and had learned to despise himself so much, that when he waited for a bus he would invariably turn his face away as the bus approached the corner, thereby giving the driver the signal to go on. Once aboard, he could not look into the faces of the passengers, so shy was he.

3    *Anxiety*. Another consequence of fear is the development of anxiety. Once you become afraid of things, you develop more fears. This is a real psychological cancer, which starts out in one spot and easily spreads to others. It can then develop

30

into fears that you don't even know the cause of. That's the start of an anxiety reaction.

One young lady had an infection on her hand which her physician speculated might be a rash brought on either by nerves or by syphilis. She knew that she was a virgin, and yet she began wondering if she had had intercourse and hadn't known about it.

This confusion and doubt over the most obvious forms of behaviour was again illustrated in the case of Mary. She and her husband had gone to a party, and under the influence of drink he had pinched her backside and made a few tasteless comments in front of the entire company. She immediately expressed her indignation in the presence of the guests and got in her car and went home. Interestingly enough, she then called me to ask if she had acted wisely. I assured her that she had conducted herself in a sensible way and that her quick action would probably assure her of not having to put up with this sort of indignity again. But the fact that she needed this assurance for such an obviously sound piece of behaviour again illustrates how doubtful the scared person is over the most common-sense decisions.

4   *Guilt.* A fairly common companion to fear is guilt. If you are usually neurotic enough to be very afraid, you are also neurotic enough to feel guilty. Ms. Nuss, for example, wanted to move to a cheaper flat after her divorce and so could not take her son's baby grand piano with her. The son, however, wailed and moaned so much at the prospect of losing his beloved instrument that she began to feel guilty over denying him something so important to him. She could have sold the piano (which was not yet paid for) and helped herself out financially. Instead, she stayed where she was, continued to pay for the old flat she could hardly afford and made payments on the piano her son certainly did not need. Her financial obligations began to wear on her and she soon became afraid of getting deeper and deeper into debt. It was always her guilt that forced her to

accept the situation and not improve it in the sensible way she had first suggested.

Fortunately this feeling of guilt can be overcome, and when it does the fear disappears also. Sue was always a rather cowardly person and felt especially intimidated while she was going through secretarial school. Maths was the one subject she found difficult to understand, even after her teacher answered all her questions. Finally, out of exasperation the teacher told her not to ask her again. At her next session with me Sue brought up this whole issue and wondered how she was ever to master this subject if she could not talk to her teacher about it. She mentioned also that she felt stupid because she was so inadequate at maths, and guilty because she kept bothering her teacher. She was afraid to insist that she had the right to have the lessons explained several times.

I counselled Sue, not against the fear, but against the guilt. I pointed out to her that there was no reason in the world why she should blame herself because she was poor in maths, since she was imperfect and everybody in the world does poorly in some areas. Apart from that, it was the teacher's obligation to teach her how to do the problems, even if it took her a hundred times to explain the subjects. I suggested that my client go back and stand up to the teacher. I assured her that she had every right in the world to expect a good performance from the teacher, and if it took longer than the teacher liked that was too bad.

Somewhat to my surprise, Sue faithfully followed my instructions to the letter. The next time her teacher showed impatience with her, Sue slowly put down her pencil, and in class with the other students present she apologized politely for being so dense in maths. She said, however, that the teacher had no moral right to become indignant over this failure. Sue said she did not like the situation any more than the teacher did. However, the teacher was being paid to teach, and if Sue wasn't able to catch on to an idea in six explanations, then she would try a seventh and an eighth, and she fully expected the teacher to go along with her.

32

This kind of confrontation worked wonders, because the teacher had more respect for her and did make every effort to see to it that Sue learned and had the explanations given to her in a patient manner. This change would have been impossible had Sue not overcome her sense of guilt.

Sometimes we confuse being assertive with being hostile. Hostility is truly an objectionable act, but being assertive is not. Sometimes in our zeal to be loving and compassionate human beings we go so far overboard that we lose our common sense and act in a most unassertive manner. Ms. Stenor discovered one day that her husband had been unfaithful to her, and that the woman involved was Ms. Stenor's best friend. At first my client was very angry over this unkind action, but then she began to feel guilty over being angry. Instead of telling her friend to get lost and that the relationship was over, Ms. Stenor turned on the charm, attempted to be a Christian and loving person, and completely surprised the woman with overtures of friendship. Much to Ms. Stenor's surprise, the woman did not desist from the relationship with Mr. Stenor, she intensified it. When that was finally understood, Ms. Stenor had had enough. She gave her husband an ultimatum and refused to have anything to do with the friend any longer. She had overcome her fear of being assertive by standing up for her rights and not feeling guilty over the need to be firm.

5 *Compulsions*. Persons who have fears also frequently develop compulsions. A compulsion is an act that a person feels he must perform or else he will experience intolerable nervousness. Sometimes such an act makes sense, but at other times is is ludicrous, such as when one struggles over something of little consequence as though it were a monumental issue.

In the case of guilt and fear, it is usually necessary to remove the guilt first and then the fear will disappear. When a compulsion is involved, however, it is important first to deal with the fear and then the compulsion will generally disappear. Jerry was a prefect at school who began to develop some of the fussiest behaviour I have ever seen. He would at times be late for his lessons or for school because he spent so much time before the mirror making certain that his tie was put on absolutely perfectly. If he discovered a spot on his trousers while on his way to school, he would return home and get another pair. Even if he was late for an appointment or for class, it made no difference. The thought of his being imperfectly dressed simply frightened him so much that he became ridiculously compulsive about his looks. The same was true of his reading and writing habits. If he thought he had read a sentence aloud incorrectly, had failed to pause at a comma, or had not properly inflected when he came to a question mark, he would read it over again as though he were reciting it on the stage. When he wrote a sentence and was not sure of the punctuation, he simply could not proceed until he was absolutely certain that the punctuation was in perfect order.

His bicycle received the same compulsive treatment that other things about him did. If he had a scratch on the mudguard, he would immediately get a daub of paint, fill it in, and then wax over the area. He was so cautious about his bicycle that he would only ride it on pavements where there was no traffic, and he would never take it through the woods because it might get scratched.

In this case it was discovered that Jerry had such a low opinion of himself that he could feel acceptable only if everything about him was in perfect shape. He would then be above criticism. The trouble with this outlook was that he believed that all he had and everything he did were projections of himself. He thought that a bad bike meant that he was a bad person, or that a crooked tie meant that he was imperfect. When I was able to show Jerry that he had every right in the world to separate things about him—including the most intimate things about his personality—from himself, he began to change. He was no longer afraid of making mistakes, since the mistakes did not reflect upon him. Before this he always thought that a mistake was like a mirror which reflected just

34

how rotten he was, and that if he spent a lot of time correcting all his mistakes he would be cleaning that mirror and then there would be no bad reflections.

Fortunately Jerry eventually learned not to judge himself by his behaviour, his bicycle, or his punctuation. He got to the point where he could ride his bike anywhere and he could write his essays without spending all evening on a few sentences.

6 *Homosexuality*. It is generally not appreciated how frequently homosexuality is intimately associated with fear. This does not mean that everyone who is a homosexual is so because he is afraid to be a heterosexual, but in a good many cases this is so. In my own experience I have found that the development of certain homosexuals goes something like the following: the child has a poor model to copy for his or her own sexual role. A boy for example, may have a father who drinks and chases women and has no close feeling for the boy. The child may, therefore, look up at his father and say within himself: "I don't want to be anything like you. You disappoint me, your behaviour is awful, and if being a man means I have to drink and be unfaithful to women, no thanks." And if the boy happens to be somewhat frail to begin with, then it is all the easier to reject his own masculinity. If he has a brother or a neighbour who also does not set a decent example as a man because all he can do is work on cars, or treat animals cruelly, then again a boy may say, "No, thanks."

Usually, along with this state of affairs, other factors are present which impair the boy's image of himself as a male. For example, perhaps his mother is always reminding him that he is a cissy, that he will never be a man like his father or his brother, and that he is going to end up someday dancing on the stage or writing poetry. So the boy becomes brainwashed into believing that the masculine role is completely out of the question for him. The men in his life convince him that to be a man you have to do certain things, and these things go against his conscience.

35

The boy grows up knowing that he is a man physically, but not emotionally. He feels he is inferior to all other men. It is a feeling he cannot stand. Secretly he would love to be masculine and to overcome this sense of inferiority that he has always had. How can he do this? Suppose that as a young man he has a romance or a love affair and does very badly at it. Perhaps the first time that he kisses a girl or becomes more intimate his pride is hurt and all of his fears about how hopeless he really is come true. Thereafter he fears being intimate with women entirely. One young man had no sexual success with a girlfriend and fared no better with a prostitute he once visited. Thereafter he decided to give up heterosexuality and go homosexual.

In overcoming the problem, it is important first of all to teach the homosexual that he still has value even if he chooses to be homosexual. He should know that cultural sexual roles and being worthwhile are not mutually exclusive, and that failure in sexual experience is not the worst thing that can happen. If he wants to give up homosexuality, and try loving women again, he may very well fail again. But heterosexual males also fail at some time or other. So what is there to be frightened of? If he would wine, dine, and romance more women (even though he might not satisfy them sexually), he could profit from any failures for which he didn't blame himself. He could study the failures, find out how he was making himself tense and worried, and then perhaps do better the next time. If he were to do this instead of blame himself for failing, he might find himself being quite an adequate male, as many homosexuals are able to demonstrate.

The whole problem of homosexuality is no longer the frightening one it once was, because we can now see that some homosexuality is essentially the result of self-hatred of one's masculine weaknesses, and fear that one will do badly with women. To overcome this we want to teach the homosexual that he has value regardless of the weaknesses he may have, and secondly, that being afraid of women and avoiding them is no way to learn how to deal successfully with them.

36

# 5
# Overcoming Fears

There are a number of strategies you can use to overcome fears. If one does not work, another can be attempted. In no case do you need to succumb to the power of a fear, since with enough dedication and knowledge it is practically possible to wipe all fears out of your life. To be as fearless as possible, however, it is perhaps most important of all to be a risk-taking person.

### Risk-taking

Unless you are willing to take a chance and to expose yourself to the very thing that you are most afraid of, you have very little chance of ever overcoming your fear. You overcome a fear because you do the thing you are afraid to do and are willing to face the dangers involved. It does not matter whether you are climbing mountains or standing up to your boss, the principle is always the same: to overcome the fear, you must take certain risks. Those people who do not take risks live in a constant state of anxiety and apprehension.

This risk-taking is easily understood when it comes to driving a car, learning to ride a motorcycle, or flying an aircraft. But there are also un-nerving risks we have to take when it comes simply to dealing with other people. Ms. Sample had been severely dominated by her tyrannical husband all her married life. Whenever he wanted something in the family to go his way, all he had to do was to bellow and stomp and storm and she immediately gave in. Eventually she was deriving so little benefit from the marriage that she began to lose interest in whether it would survive. She came for counselling to see what she could do about straightening out this relationship.

I told her that she would have to learn to stand up to this fellow even though he threatened to beat her up. She would have to take the risk which she had been avoiding for twenty years in her marriage and finally do the one thing she was most afraid to do—*not* give in to her husband. She had rights as a human being and as a wife, and unless she stood up for them she would never get them. This would be a risky task, but she was going to have to learn to do this or their marriage would never improve.

The first time she decided to stand up to him was when her husband had a go at one of their children over a minor mistake. In the past she was always afraid to tell him what was on her mind. The few times she did register a complaint he became so loud and threatening that she immediately became a mouse. This time, however, she decided to tell him to get off the child's back and not to make so much of the little mistake the boy had made. Before speaking up, she recognized that she had a strong desire just to keep silent and to walk out of the room. But this time she felt she simply had to take the risk or else it would go on this way forever. She finally told him off, and for a moment he was shocked into silence. He quickly rallied, however, and became even more threatening. He pushed her around and told her in no uncertain terms that she had better never again correct him in his dealings with the children.

She lost her nerve. She became quiet and backed off. When I saw her in counselling the following week I assured her that she had done quite well up to a point, but that she had evaded the risk involved in standing up to him a second time. It was risky to offer him this much opposition, but it nevertheless had to be done. I encouraged her to stand up for her rights regardless of what he would do. If he became violent, she could call the police.

In time, Ms. Sample became more and more risk-taking and began to assert herself in more and more ways, even though it occasionally caused some violent scenes. But her husband could begin to detect that his days of bullying her were finally over and that if he wanted to get along with her, he would simply have to give in to some of her desires.

38

At times failure to take risks can lead to sad consequences. I recall the case of a woman who wanted to adopt a foster child and even submitted the papers for this process. In the meantime, however, she began to think about the possibility of being rejected because she had a history of poverty in her family and her educational background was rather limited. Rather than carry this issue to its logical end, she became fearful of being turned down and decided that she would not go through with the adoption plans after all.

The official from the social services reported to my client that the adoption had actually been granted and she could have had the child had she not changed her mind. How sad. Is this not often the way we behave? And how foolish it is. If my client had gone ahead and taken the risk and failed, she would have been no worse off than she ended up when she refused to take the risk, thereby losing nothing. By taking the risk, she would always have had the possibility in the future of gaining something. This, it seems to me, is the most important point to remember about risk-taking: to take risks frequently means that you will succeed *sometimes*. Never to take risks means that you *almost never* succeed. Which course of action should you take? One course of action has a 5 per cent possibility of success, and another has a 1 per cent possibility of success. As low as the former may be, it is always better than the latter.

The first step then in overcoming fear is to stop making mountains out of molehills and talking yourself into thinking you are about to undergo an enormous risk if you make the next move. Instead, stick your neck out and take a chance. Life is filled with risks, and if you choose to retreat from every challenge, I can assure you that you will be bored to death. If you never risk driving a car, you miss out on an enormous amount of enjoyment. If you never risk being rejected, you will never have a date or a partner. If you never risk asking for a job, you will never be employed. Practically anything of value requires that one take a risk of either being rejected or hurt. So be it. It is the price we must all pay. But it is not a price that is impossible or unreasonable to pay.

> *"It is more important to do than to do well."*

Albert Ellis said this and I quote him because it is a very important statement. It means that you do not have to wait until your performance is perfect before you engage in an activity. It is perfectly O.K. to perform badly, because you will eventually gain the mastery you seek. It is virtually impossible to do something perfectly, or even well, the first time you try. Of the millions of complex tasks we have all mastered, isn't it true that they were all done quite badly at first and only improved because we continued to do them badly, but less and less so as we practised?

Still, millions of people will refuse to try an activity simply because they will not do it well. They believe that everything they do must be perfect and that they are worthless people if they do not behave perfectly at all times. What nonsense!

To remedy this condition, stop and ask yourself what it is that you are afraid to do and then see whether you can get yourself to do it. No matter how badly, do it! Are you a bad letter writer? Then write more letters. Only by doing so can you eventually write letters well. Are you afraid of appearing on the stage and would you like not to be afraid? Then get on the stage and try your best, no matter how poor it is. Accept small acting roles from your local amateur theatre. Accept requests for speeches. Get up in public gatherings and ask questions of the speaker. Do the thing you are afraid of. Do not care too much whether or not you are doing well. Eventually, as you do better, the fear will simply have to diminish.

Mastery of a task comes partly through practice. Our saying that practice makes perfect is not really quite accurate. More appropriate is the proverb, "Practice makes the master." This is the point that we must emphasize. If we have not mastered something yet, we are really saying that we have not practised it enough. To master an activity, we have to (*a*) practise it; (*b*) examine the performance to find out where we are lacking; (*c*) change; and (d) practise it again. We will eventually get to the point where we are continually improving because of this critical approach and doing the activity better and better.

If we do not follow this piece of advice, we automatically build up enormous fears. For example, if you feel awkward at parties because you don't know how to make light chatter and you tend to end up being ignored, then spend more time analyzing what it is that you are doing that makes it an unpleasant evening. Instead of allowing yourself to become increasingly afraid, simply remind yourself that only by going to more parties, regardless of how badly you socialize, will you be put on the right course. Sooner or later you'll get to the point where you will feel more and more comfortable mingling as they do at informal gatherings, and you may even get to the point where you enjoy it. But you must attend more of them, no matter how badly you are faring currently. To do otherwise is to invite increasing fear and doubt and retreat from activity.

## Challenge the irrational beliefs

Fundamentally we become afraid by talking ourselves into believing that because something is dangerous or fearsome we ought to think about it, focus upon it, dwell upon it, and worry about it constantly. If we did not believe such nonsense, it would be impossible to become afraid. Most people will readily agree with this until they come up against a special activity which they will make an exception, saying, "But this is so serious an issue that I ought to think about it and worry over it even though I don't usually do this with other issues."

There are technically no exceptions. One does not need to be afraid of anything. To achieve the complete absence of fear is, of course, difficult. But it can almost be done if one vigorously challenges the neurotic idea that we ought to be afraid of things because they are unpleasant and the idea that events happening outside our lives have the ability to upset us. When my clients insist they are not neurotic just because they express a fear or a worry over something that is happening or may happen, I point out to them that in every case they are ignoring a hundred other dangers around them which are a great deal worse than the ones they are presently focusing upon. If they are to be consistent about their fears, then they will worry about aircraft dropping on them or atomic bombs going off, about being poisoned by botulism, or being shot or robbed on the street.

This is the kind of discussion I once had with a young fellow who had invested about £7,000 in a business and was rightly afraid that he might lose it. He was by no means wealthy. He had taken most of his savings and speculated rather rashly. It was small wonder, therefore, that he thought of this night and day. It was beginning to affect him physically and he was worried and depressed.

I was finally able to show him that the £7,000 might very well go up in smoke, but that it was hardly the end of the world. He was a young fellow and would see another £7,000 for certain before many years rolled by. Furthermore he had profited enormously by this foolish venture because he was probably a great deal wiser as a result of the experience. Most of all he still had his health and his job, and he would only be down by an amount which he could probably recoup in a number of years. Still, he clung to the idea that this was a terrible thing that had happened to him and that he ought to think about it and worry over it and fret upon it all the time. For some weeks he remained totally unchanged. Finally I got him to think vigorously about his idea that he *ought* to be upset simply because something unpleasant was happening to him. Only when he recognized this as a neurotic idea did he begin to change.

People are always insisting that when they can predict dire consequences they have a right to become awfully upset. The point is—why? Why should people be terribly distraught simply because unpleasant things will happen to them? That possibility exists every morning of our lives. We get up and we haven't the foggiest notion of what painful things might happen to us today. Should we focus upon them at all times? Don't we have any faith in our ability to survive these things? Must we be upset by unpleasant events? Don't we in fact have a choice as to whether or not we will be upset? Of course we do. It simply is not true that we must constantly focus on the dangers we are in once we have done whatever we can to reduce them. At that point it is a great deal better to distract yourself and get your mind off the situation rather than to dwell upon it at all times.

Distraction is at times one of the better things you can do about nervousness. I vividly recall a friend of mine who was being sued rather heavily, certainly beyond the coverage of his insurance policy. However, he hired a lawyer and then did not allow anyone in the family to bring up the subject again. It was simply something no one talked about—the less said, the better. Because no one talked about it they found it easier to distract themselves from this menacing problem and they eventually got involved in other things. It took months before the case came to court and it was eventually settled without any great harm to him. However, had he not forced his attention onto other matters, he would have been a very nervous young man.

He diverted his attention by juggling figures in his head whenever he thought of the lawsuit. If this didn't work, he simply got on the phone and called someone, or went to a cinema, or read a book. Anything was fair game for distraction. If he did not find the distraction successful at first, he simply stayed with it and pretended to become absorbed in the subject until finally he *was* absorbed for a while. The longer he did this the more he found himself being directed well away from his main problem and this immediately gave him relief.

It is impossible to be upset about something unless you are thinking about it. If your thoughts are on something pleasant rather than something unpleasant, it is impossible to be disturbed, no matter what kind of pressures you are under. If you are thinking about a fine meal or a football game instead of the lawsuit, then you can have one hundred lawsuits facing you and you will not be disturbed by any of them, simply because your thoughts will be elsewhere. To be upset by things, we have

43

to be thinking about them. It is the same with vision. If I turn my eyes away from something unpleasant, I will not be able to see it and pleasant things at the same time. I can look in only one direction at a time. Therefore, I can exclude anything irritating if I want to. Mentally I can do the same thing. If I do not like what I am thinking about, I can focus elsewhere. If I am truly focusing upon something pleasant, then I cannot be upset by something unpleasant.

It will be difficult for you at first to challenge the neurotic idea that you ought to be upset over ominous events. However, that idea *can* be beaten and with constant effort *can* be dispelled until you find yourself simply not believing it. Then you can face serious issues in a very calm way.

## Exposure

All too often it is forgotten that a broad exposure to life tends to reduce the number of fears you have. The more you know about the world, the more comfortable you tend to be in it. People who have flown in an aircraft a thousand times do not have the same nervousness as a person who is taking his first flight. Someone who has given many speeches can enjoy what the novice dreads. But in addition to the obvious exposure which travel and experience give you, there is another benefit, the comparison it gives you between your life and the lives of others. For example, if you have been afraid to do something for some time, you may overcome this fear very quickly when you see others doing it rather easily. Ms. Roe was a person who profited by a sudden spurt of travel. She and her husband had been homelovers while the children were growing up, but once they left the nest the parents were free to do quite a bit of travelling. Only then did she see how other men treated their wives, and this encouraged her to stand up for her rights and to begin to see her role as wife in a more equal manner. It would probably never have happened had she not had that exposure from travel.

When you get the opportunity, try to experience all that you safely can from any situation you find yourself in. If you do not like eating chocolate-covered ants and you find yourself at a party where they are being served, try a few, even if you are positive that the whole thing is a silly pretence at being fashionable. It would not be difficult to eat almost anything else you had to eat if you could manage to get down a few of these ants. I well remember several long hikes that I took when I was in the Army. One was a five-mile forced march and another was a twenty-mile forced march. In addition, I was trained to bivouac out in the open and to work and sleep in very uncomfortable weather. Later, during the war in Europe and back in the United States in my civilian career as a graduate student, I found this training and exposure came in quite handy. I did not hesitate to do some camping in wild country and to take long walks, because I had similar prior experiences. Having already gone through an experience once, I was not the least bit fearful of what might happen the second time.

## Relaxation techniques

When some people become nervous and tense they begin to breathe rapidly, and this causes more oxygen to be absorbed into the bloodstream than is desirable. In fact, it makes them dizzy and this leads to their feeling more upset, and more frightened that something bad is happening.

A relaxed person can obviously not be a nervous person. Therefore, when you find yourself becoming tense, relax mentally and you will cancel out the physical tension. There are a number of relaxation techniques being practised these days, and the most popular currently is probably transcendental meditation. This is a technique whereby the individual attempts to meditate fifteen to twenty minutes twice a day with eyes closed while he focuses on a mantra—a word, the sound of which he was taught to focus upon. As his mind wanders onto the cares of the day he has to pull himself back to focusing upon the word, and the more successful he is at this, the more relaxed he eventually becomes. He transcends ordinary thought and is attuned to the so-called source of thought. Those people who practise transcendental meditation claim that after doing this for a number of months they become much more peaceful and relaxed individuals.

In all likelihood this is effective because it permits the person to direct his attention to a harmless word rather than to all the troubles he is experiencing that day. I wonder if this is not the same as the diversion technique I have already described and which differs from it very little in theory: i.e., anything that diverts you from your troubles will give you relief.

At night, when you are ready for bed, a good way to relieve your tensions would be to lie down in a comfortable position and relax your entire body in one of two ways. The first way: simply focus upon a small segment of your body at a time and tell it to relax. When that part is relaxed, move on to another section. In this fashion you might start with the scalp and tell it to relax and then go to the forehead and down to the ear, the cheeks, the nose, the eyes, the lips, the chin, and so on all the way down to the toes.

The second relaxation technique: focus on a part of your body in the same way as in the previous method, but tense the muscles first for several seconds and then relax them. Then go on to another section and tense that vigorously for a few seconds and then relax it. Some feel this requires more energy and actually induces more relaxation.

Yoga is another excellent way to calm down and to relax the body. The stretching exercises called for in yoga and the breathing and meditation that are usually employed all have a very soothing effect upon the body.

Sitting in moments of silent prayer has of course been known for centuries as an excellent way to bring peace and tranquillity to a troubled soul. Millions of people have faced overwhelming crises through prayer as a source of strength and hope.

### The back-off tendency

A person who has been afraid for a long time is usually not

46

going to overcome his fear in a short time. He will tend to think of himself as still having that fear when really he has already mastered it. If you were to mention to him that he had managed a certain task very well, he might reject the compliment, because this would imply that he is now expected to face every task as though he had no fear of it. Shirley was a young girl who had a number of personality problems, among which were not being very sexy and being depressed. As she began working on both of these problems she occasionally got compliments from her friends about how much more attractive she was becoming and how much more cheerful she appeared. However, she did not feel pleased when these compliments were made; rather, she felt tense and threatened. She felt as though she now had to live up to the responsibility of continuing to change as she had done, and she was afraid that she might let down the people who were complimenting her.

It is important, therefore, not to be too enthusiastic in complimenting a person who is overcoming a fear. He may misinterpret your compliment to mean that perfect behaviour will henceforth be expected from him. He might eventually, of course, be able to behave in a confident manner practically all of the time, but at the moment the compliment is made he may not trust himself to live up to such an expectation. Usually he is doing a great deal better than he thinks, but just can't believe it. He is very much like a child learning to ride a bicycle. The child thinks his dad is holding on to the saddle in order to prevent him from falling. But every so often the dad—who is running along with the child—will let go of the cycle, and the child will be riding on his own but not know it. When the boy is told later that he rode half a block without his dad's even touching the bike he might become quite frightened rather than pleased, because he realizes that he is now on his own and he may not always be able to avoid falling. People who are afraid and who lean upon others to help them with their fears are not always quick to give them up, because to do so means they have become independent, something fearful people are not particularly eager to do.

## Face your fears gradually

One of the worst things you can do in the attempt to overcome a fear is to face the whole thing, head on, at one time. The impact of such an experience can be so great that it can work in reverse and make you ten times more afraid than you were originally. Generally, the best way to face a fear is to face it at a distance and a little bit at a time. You can be quite accustomed to a dangerous situation if you take it in small doses.

A child who has a fear of water should not be grabbed by the sleeve and thrown into a pool. Though this sometimes works, it is not always a wise technique. People can become so frightened that they become unmanageable if forced to face their fears all at once. Or suppose a child wanted to overcome his fear of school. It would be much more sensible for him to ride around the school on his bike. Then after he did that for a few days he could walk into the hallways and come out whenever he felt tense. After this he might visit his classroom or some of the offices and go in and chat a bit with some of the people present. After this he might go to his lessons for very short periods of time, with the understanding that he could leave whenever he felt very uncomfortable.

As this is mastered he could stay in the classroom for longer and longer periods, pushing himself if necessary to tolerate just a little bit more fear. By extending the time in this way he could get to the point where he could stay in one class for one period and then eventually a whole day. The important thing in this technique is that the fear be approached gradually rather than hastily. If it is faced hastily, the person pays the consequences.

In one case I had a student return to a class that he feared. He had been told to leave when he felt uncomfortable. However, he managed to stay through three classes by sheer will-power and found the experience so unpleasant that he could not return the next day at all. This would not have happened if he had not told himself that he needed to stay. He

48

exposed himself to too much too fast. The lesson to be learned from this is that one should take it easy and make progress slowly.

## How to overcome catastrophizing

The first step you must perform in order to become upset is to make mountains out of molehills. The moment you tell yourself that something is *awful* or *terrible*, or that you are facing a *catastrophe*, you are going to become disturbed. If you blame yourself for that frustration or pity yourself or pity someone else, you will shape that frustration into a depression. On the other hand, if you blame someone else for what you are going through, then you will shape that frustration into a feeling of anger and hatred. But if you just leave it alone and continue to worry about it and imagine the worst happening to you because you are facing an unpleasant situation, you will not reshape that frustration into anything but simply leave it as a catastrophe. The net result to you will be fear, worry, nervousness, uneasiness, and some general feeling of tension at the very least.

To overcome this important first step in *any* emotional disturbance it is extremely important to question whether or not the thing you are facing is in fact a catastrophe. If you can persuade yourself that the issue you are dealing with is not really all that serious, then you are bound to calm down. But if you continue to tell yourself that you are facing a life-and-death issue, you will be terribly disturbed.

There are two things we can do with these catastrophizing situations. On the one hand, we can convince ourselves that they are actually not catastrophes to begin with, and secondly, if we cannot convince ourselves honestly that we are not facing a life-and-death matter, then we had better convince ourselves that—even if it is a very serious situation—there is really no need to become terribly disturbed over it, since that only makes our situation worse. In either case one does not need to be bowled over because a crisis, either real or imagined, is occurring. Fortunately most of the frustrations that enter our lives are hardly crises at all, and when we have looked at them more carefully and allowed some time to pass we usually judge these things much better. We usually come to realize that we are not in such bad shape as we thought initially.

This is what happened to John, a college student. During the Vietnam conflict he was ordered to go to his draft induction centre for a physical examination. When he got there and saw the calibre of people he would be living and socializing with, it made him almost sick to his stomach. He came from a rather selective background—all members of his family were highly educated and had travelled a lot. The men he encountered at the draft centre were unsophisticated, with ordinary backgrounds and the usual education.

He began to have nightmares at the mere thought of living with a group of uneducated fellows who could talk about nothing but their cars and their gangs for the next two years.

John took this matter so seriously that he became greatly agitated over the possibility that he might have to share his life with such people. He nearly became a nervous wreck. Each day he was telling himself: "It's going to *kill* me if I have to be training with those fellows. I just *can't stand* it. How am I going to talk to those knuckleheads about their motors and their gangs?" This kind of self-propagandizing made him increasingly nervous to the point where he had to seek counselling.

During one of my first sessions with him I said something like the following: "John, why can't you tolerate being in company that you don't like? Millions of other people have done this all their lives. I don't see why you can't. You keep saying you can't and of course that's why you finally believe you can't do it. But if you were to question that nonsense, that it's going to kill you if you are with them, you simply could not believe it for very long. And who knows, you might in fact have a very interesting two years if you would open your eyes and get to know this group of people. Simply because they have less experience than you do is not an indication that they aren't talented, artistic, and equally intelligent."

"I thought of that too, doctor, but whenever I really think deeply about spending twenty-four months in the Army in that kind of environment I just go bananas."

"But that's only because you keep telling yourself it's so awful."

"But it *is* awful. I just know I'll just go nuts if I have to be trained."

My immediate response to this was, "But that's only because you think you have no choice and that you *have* to be upset about it."

"Yes, that's exactly what I think. And isn't that right?"

"No. *Why* must you be upset just because you're not going to enjoy the next two years of your life? You act as if you're going to face a firing squad. It's hardly that. But even if it were, why would you have to be upset by it?"

"Why would I have to be upset by facing a firing squad?"

"Yes, I maintain it is perfectly possible to face a firing squad without losing your mind. I can recall an instance when I watched on television the chief of police of Havana jauntily tilt his hat over his head as he walked up against the wall before a firing squad and was shot with a smile on his face. That man didn't lose his mind just before he died. He must have told himself, 'Well, if I'm going to die, let's do it gracefully.' You, on the other hand, think that because you are facing something unpleasant you *have* to worry about it, you *must* be upset about it, and you *should* be terribly frightened of it."

John then replied, "So you actually mean that it is possible for me not only to face Army training but, for example, to face an artillery barrage or a charge by the enemy without losing my nerve or becoming terribly panicky?"

"Of course it's possible. Don't tell me that throughout history men haven't in fact enjoyed this kind of danger. I don't deny that this was mixed with feelings of apprehension and downright fear, but most of them never lost control of themselves. You are acting like you're facing a monster every day, when all you have to do is live around a few fellows that you're not particularly fond of for two years. And that's hardly a comparison. If you hadn't made a wholly impossible thing out of being trained and convinced yourself neurotically that just because you don't like something that it's the end of the world, you wouldn't be in the state you're in right now."

As it turned out, he was able to get a deferment, the war ended, and he was never called up. This is another example of how frequently the things we worry about never really come to pass at all.

Another example of how to overcome one's tendency to catastrophize, no matter what the situation, was given to me when I counselled a troubled young woman. She had a poor family background and was simply trying to understand herself and her history so that she could live a less confused and stressful life. She had apparently been sexually manipulated by her father when she was a child and other advances were still being made by him from time to time. She was haunted by her inability to put a stop to them. When she went to a shop she would develop the strange feeling that she was walking around partly undressed. She would blush and immediately make her exit for her car and go home. Asking me what she could do about it, I immediately responded, "Lump it."

By this I meant that the more she made of the symptom, the stronger it would get. The only way she could eventually see that symptom disappear entirely was for her simply to accept it as it was, not to fight it, but to ignore it if possible. She was not to leave a shop at any time simply because she had that feeling that she was half naked. She should in fact stay there and do her shopping and pretend that nothing was happening. No matter how embarrassed she felt, she was told to stick it out until she could see that nothing serious would happen even if she did have that feeling.

At first this whole idea disturbed her. But the more she questioned the awfulness of that feeling, the more relief she began to feel. It was not too long before she stopped catastrophizing completely and did in fact see the disappearance of the symptom. Occasionally, however, it would come back, especially if she saw a man at the store who reminded her of her father. At those times, however, she just calmly told herself: "So I have that feeling again. Why should I get all upset about it? It isn't awful. It isn't going to kill anybody. What difference does it make if I have a feeling that I'm half nude? That's my neurotic problem. And if I don't make a big deal out of it, no one else will know about it. So I'll just go ahead and ignore the whole thing and buy my tomatoes."

This is essentially what I have been stressing about neurotic symptoms that are unwelcomed and have a way of persisting in one's behaviour. The more we try to fight to get rid of them, the worse they get. On the other hand, if we ignore them, pay no attention to them, and can manage to accept them for what they are, the less hold they have over us.

### Things get worse first

Whenever you attempt to change your behaviour, do not expect the improvement curve to be a straight line. Instead, expect the graph of improvement to go up and down and sometimes to take pretty deep dips. If you are not prepared for reverses as you are recovering, you are going to get panicky. You will think that you haven't learned a thing, that the old symptoms are coming back just as strong as they ever were, and that things are getting worse. If you have this attitude, then you completely misunderstand the nature of learning. Learning usually takes place in an erratic way, and you never know from one time to the next just how you are going to do. If you accept that, then you won't be so hard on yourself or be so surprised when you do less well than you had hoped—whether you are learning to play tennis or overcoming your worries and fears.

You can especially expect things to get worse if you have to face a fear that you have been avoiding all of your life. The closer you get to doing the thing that you are afraid of, the worse your behaviour will probably be. This is especially true with people who are trying to grow up, who are trying to find their independence, and who have previously leaned upon others all of their lives. To get them to face their difficulties is an enormous task and usually scares the very daylights out of them. I recall the case of an elderly woman whom I shall call Betty, who, although very bright, was vegetating in her old age. I knew that she would feel a lot better if she could be active, get a part-time job, or work as a volunteer. So I suggested that she go out and risk failure, risk rejection, and prove to herself and the world that she was really not a dependent weakling. The mere suggestion was so threatening to her that as I continued to urge her to do something about her spare time her behaviour began to get noticeably worse. Although she usually sat in her chair when we talked in my office, she now began to pace back and forth. She had been in the habit of driving to my office for her appointments. Now she insisted that she was too tense to drive and she was taking a cab instead. She had not needed tranquillizers at all for some time, but at this point she had her doctor prescribe drugs for her. And lastly, she definitely began to complain to me about suicidal thoughts, something that she had not seriously expressed for a long time.

All this behaviour indicates the increasing threat of the possibility of failure and a plea for an escape from facing the real fear that is the root of the problem. This is a normal and natural development in the life of anyone overcoming a fear and should be anticipated.

I tried to reassure my client that she was acting in an understandable way, since she had avoided seeking a job for many years. The mere thought of getting back into the labour market was frightening her, and she was trying to get out of it by these manoeuvres. I kindly reminded her that she did not have to do this; she could regain her skills at a slow pace, and even if that failed it wouldn't be the end of the world. In the final analysis it was more important to do, than to do well. And if she did take a job and it lasted for only a day or two, she would at least have learned something while she was on the job.

This would be good preparation for her when she looked for her second job. In short, even though she was very tense about not doing well it was still quite necessary that she face the issue rather than avoid it.

### Spontaneous recovery

Now that we have discussed a number of different ways to overcome worry, nervousness, and fear, let me offer a word of warning. There is a strong tendency for neurotic symptoms to return after you think you have rid yourself of them. This is called spontaneous recovery, because it seems that symptoms return almost by themselves. You may have done remarkably well, for example, about talking to strangers or not being afraid of going on the dance floor. Then one day you attempt to go on the dance floor and you realize that you are scared silly. This fear may come completely without warning, and you may assume that you are stuck with the same old problem, just as bad as it ever was, and that it will take just as long to get rid of it again as it took the first time.

What you must realize when a symptom returns spontaneously is that you have simply been careless about fighting it. It was for this reason that it crept up on you and suddenly stood before you again after you had conquered it for days or months. All you need to do is to get back on the job and beat down that mental nonsense until you no longer believe (a) that you ought to be terribly upset about something, (b) that worrying helps, and (c) that the more you focus on some dreaded event, the better it is. If you challenge such notions immediately, you are bound to regain quick control over that symptom, whether it be worry or fear, and you will find yourself getting back to where you were before it suddenly reappeared.

Each time you have to fight your way back to calmness you will find that it takes less and less time to recover from one of these spontaneous slips. They can occur a number of times before you have finally mastered the fear or the worry so

55

completely that you are, for all practical purposes, not disturbed by them any longer.

Nothing succeeds like success, and when you have once learned to calm yourself or to rid yourself of worrying you will find that each time it will be that much easier. Therefore, work hard at it and assure yourself over and over that it is completely possible to rid yourself of most of your fears and worries. Be careful not to make the mistake of thinking that this is only a matter of positive thinking. This is not just a matter of giving yourself a sales pitch so that you will feel good and convince yourself that all is well in this world. That is not the case at all. I have never suggested that you should wear rose-coloured glasses so that you can go through life assuming that everything is going to be wonderful. My objection has been that in most instances we look at the world with dark-coloured glasses and make each experience appear worse than it really is. In those few cases when matters are really quite serious, there is still no good reason why we should become unduly upset. We are going to be hurt and frustrated in the future, to be sure. The only way to avoid that is to die. Every living creature has to go through some suffering; if it isn't today, it will be tomorrow. There is no reason, however, to be terrified or get nervous and worried about these possibilities if we remind ourselves (a) that most frustrations are really not as bad as we think they are and (b) that even if some are that bad, we do not have to lose our minds over them and thus make matters worse.

### Reward or penalize yourself

Others are usually too busy to pay much attention to how you are doing on your self-improvement programme. It's nice if you have someone cheering you on and giving you a pat on the back every time you talk to a new girl, try a new high dive, or throw a party. However, if you are not getting rewards from others, give them to yourself. Here's how to use rewards and penalties on your own behalf.

Let's say you're afraid to speak up in small groups (more

than four or five people). When you force yourself to make the effort, give yourself a reward of something you truly value, such as a night out, a new shirt, or a fine bottle of wine. But each time you fail to fill your assignment, give yourself a penalty, one you have decided will really hurt, such as spending an evening with a boring neighbour, washing the car, or exercising for one hour.

If you will be fair with yourself, you will find your eagerness to give yourself more rewards and fewer penalties shaping your behaviour in the desired direction.

## *Rational-emotive imagery*

REI, short for Rational-Emotive Imagery, means that you can help yourself overcome fears if you will imagine them at their worst and take sharp notice of how you feel while doing so. Then you are to imagine, as vividly as you can, how you would tolerate the fear until your disturbance subsides. This amounts to rehearsing the dreaded event so often that you become familiar with it and rob it of its danger.

For example, a woman who wants a divorce but is afraid she wouldn't be able to stand it would be asked to imagine herself already divorced. She would think of the evenings at home alone, cooking for herself, going to shows by herself, hearing spooky noises in the dead of night, and so forth. When she fully gets the picture as she imagines it at its worst, she then tries to deal with each of these painful images.

First, she imagines herself getting busy in the evening, doing interesting things, having friends over, starting a new romance, buying locks for the doors and windows, etc. In short, she tries to live through an event as realistically as she can, but tries to fight it at the same time. The REI exercise can give you confidence in the future because your imagination has foreseen most of what you will deal with. It is recommended that you go through an REI exercise for two ten-minute periods every day until the fear is dispelled.

# 6

## Pitfalls to Recovery

Even if you have understood the previous twelve steps to overcoming your fears, you may still find yourself being fearful because you are not aware of some of the common pitfalls you might run into. Unless you avoid these, all your best efforts may be frustrated.

### Being afraid of what you will find in counselling

Among the biggest fears that you might have about overcoming your fear or worry is what you may find out about yourself if you go into therapy. Some people have the most awful notions of what takes place in a psychotherapist's office. They make excuses and rationalizations in the most fantastic ways to protect themselves against coming and talking to someone about their problems.

This is most regrettable, since in most cases there is absolutely nothing terrible to be revealed, nothing that the psychotherapist hasn't heard before. In any one day he listens to all manner of suffering. Whatever embarrassing tales, humiliations, failures, and imperfections you may have are not going to surprise him in the slightest.

If you are not afraid of how your story will affect your psychotherapist, then you may be afraid of how uncovering the truth about yourself will affect you. But this too is a sad misconception people have about psychotherapy. They are all so certain that when they start to talk about themselves and begin to understand the truth about themselves, they are going to find something deep and ugly in their souls which they had better let lie rather than face. What total nonsense this is! Basically most people are hardworking, decent citizens who try to make the best of their lives and offend others as little as possible. The idea that there is something hideous inside them that's going to come out in therapy is not realistic.

Most of those who suffer from depression, anger, or fear are that way because they were literally taught and trained to act in neurotic ways. The people who raised them taught them how to be scared, how to be a worrier, how to be angry and depressed. You have been learning those lessons all your life and most of you have been rather good students. The real problem is that you had poor teachers, not that there was anything seriously wrong with you. When you go to counselling, you are asking to be taught more sensible lessons than you learned in the past. This means that therapy can become an extremely exciting and uplifting experience in which you can finally have all the neurotic ideas cleaned out. Shortly after you enter therapy you may find yourself feeling more relieved than you ever thought possible. For example, if you have blamed yourself most of your life and thought that you were worthless because you didn't live up to your parents' expectations, you might find the therapist telling you that you have every right in the world to still think well of yourself even if you know you disappointed your parents. How can that be a frightening experience? How could you not like being told that you are a worthwhile person no matter what you have done? This is the kind of healthy and uplifting help one gets from good counselling. The whole idea is to make you a strong, healthy, and untroubled human being, not a tense, neurotic, and fretful person.

Unfortunately the cinema and some of the old methods of psychoanalysis have tended to scare people away from counselling because they thought they would have to lie down on a couch and dig up every last remnant of their childhood memories in order to overcome their present difficulties. This is no longer the way counselling works. In any typical day I infrequently ask about childhood. Most of the time I focus upon what the person is suffering from now and what he will have to do now to undisturb himself. This means we focus upon what he is thinking of when he gets upset today and what he would have to think about if he wants to deal with that today.

59

Sometimes this relates back to his childhood. If so, it is important to talk about it. The focus is very seldom on childhood for any length of time, however. It is always the current situation that good therapy focuses upon.

Instead of being afraid of psychotherapy, seek it. Seek therapy if you are uncomfortable and want some relief. The kind of therapy that is being practised today is more concerned with the problems that presently disturb people. It aims to help them understand what is wrong and to do what they can to cope with it. This is the type of therapy that I have been discussing all through this book.

## Self-fulfilling prophecies

Another pitfall in overcoming your nervousness and fears is the pessimistic outlook that you may adopt by predicting that you won't succeed. All you have to do most of the time to ensure failure is to predict that you will fail. When you say to yourself that you are not going to do well at something, you immediately slow down in the energy you apply. You begin to think of yourself as a failure and to imagine all manner of things going wrong. In short, you are failure-orientated. Then when you have failed you pat yourself on the back for being such a good predictor. The truth of the matter is, however, that you did not fail because you were unable to do the task, but rather because you *made* the prediction come true.

I know of a young man who is bright enough to go to college and to be a leader among men. Yet this same fellow has done nothing but fail because he continually predicts that he will fail. Often he does not even attempt a task because he is certain he will fail. This in itself assures his failure. For example, he was certain that he would not be able to do enough revision work in his last year in high school, so he refused to even attempt it. He therefore did not pass his exams—just as he predicted. It never occurred to him that if he had tried he might not have failed, even though the chances of his failing were great. But all the time he pretended (whether he knew it or not) that he had a crystal ball which could accurately predict the outcome of all of his actions. This is the way it went every time he applied for a job. He would destroy his hopes to the point where he knew that he wasn't going to get it. Then he would walk into a grocery store or a shop with that attitude showing on his face, in his body movements, and in his voice. The head of the establishment would quickly get the idea that he was a loser, that he had little self-confidence, and that he might not even want the job, because he didn't give the impression of chasing it. Of course the employer would reject him, and my client would come home and assure everybody that what he predicted had come true. What he did not realize was that, in an automatic and unconscious way, he deliberately and diligently worked to defeat himself. He made his prediction come true. When we practise this sort of self-fulfilling prophecy, we are often amazed at how well we hit the target. What we don't always realize is that when we make such a prophecy we work hard to be sure that it comes out exactly as we predicted, even if the prediction goes against us.

Therefore, if you take this attitude in tackling your worries and your fears, no matter how hard you try it won't work. If on the other hand you take the attitude that you are not sure whether it will work but that trying is more important than succeeding, you may find that in a great many cases you will succeed.

## Failure to challenge irrational fears

Overcoming your worries and fears is all but impossible unless you also vigorously attack the neurotic misconceptions that create these worries and fears. I hope I have demonstrated that the neurotic reactions connected with nervousness in all its various forms come not from the situations we find ourselves in at all, but from the way we think about things. Therefore, if you do not attack your belief in at least two neurotic ideas, you will never overcome your neurotic reactions.

The first neurotic idea that you will want to challenge is the idea that outside events can upset us. Remember always that it is our *thinking* about things which disturbs us, not the things themselves. Not since you were a child was it ever true that you were made nervous or tense by anything. It makes no difference who says otherwise. Consider them mistaken, even if they are persons of great authority. To say that outside events disturb us directly simply is not true. Such events disturb us only indirectly. It is we who permit unhappy events to make us unhappy.

The second neurotic idea that you must challenge if you want to become more stable is the idea that it is important to think about a danger just because you are in a dangerous situation. More explicitly, it is the idea that you should constantly think of, dwell upon, and worry over a frightening or fearful situation if that is where you find yourself. Always question exactly why it is proper that you worry about something simply because it is threatening you. What is to be accomplished by constant focusing upon certain dangers? Always remember that of all the dangers you are thinking about, there are many more which you are totally ignoring and that some of them are far more dangerous than the one you are fretting over.

### Giving up too soon

When you study what people have been able to do once they have set their minds to it, there is simply no excuse for giving up until one is absolutely convinced that a task is impossible. To get that kind of conviction one would first have to do a great many things to prove the point.

We have all heard of people who paint or draw by putting a paintbrush between their teeth or between their toes because they have no hands or arms. Many blind persons fix radio and television sets, tune pianos and even change piano strings, a very complicated feat even for a man with eyes. Bob Richards, the Olympic champion and minister, mentions a man who had set a record for kicking a football the farthest. He is a man without toes. Richards also mentions that at one time he wanted to become a marathon runner but found the going tough after eight miles and decided this was not for him. He apparently gave up too soon. He later discovered that there was a man who had entered twenty-five marathons in a single year and he had neither toes, nor heels, nor the balls of his feet.

Giving up too soon simply reflects a person's *attitude*. He thinks he cannot do something, and because he keeps on believing this he does stop too soon and he does fail. It seems to him then that his predictions are always coming true and that he is consequently pretty smart. What he does not understand, however, is that he is again fulfilling his own prophecies that he will not be able to accomplish a certain task. This of course does not prove his point; it only proves what his brainwashing will accomplish.

In overcoming your worries and fears, many of the instructions you have been given in this book will sound ridiculous and strange. You will find yourself not succeeding with them from time to time. Rather than give up, stay with it in the firm knowledge that thousands of others have used these instructions and have stopped their excessive worrying and have overcome their fears. Just because you aren't able to manage this all the time is no reason to give up and slide back into your old neurotic patterns. If you will fight your tendencies to give up, you are bound to keep it up. This in itself will eventually give you some success, and success will spur you on to new heights of achievement.

### What is improvement?

People give up at times because they do not recognize improvement when they get it. Too many of us insist that a performance must be near perfect before we can consider the question of improvement. The fact that behaviour may have improved slightly and that this time there is one less mistake seems too unimpressive for most people to notice. Change must of necessity come in great leaps before anyone notices that there

is a change. As long as you insist upon great improvement
before you will be satisfied, you are doomed to failure.
Improvement of complex behaviour comes in small steps.
Unless you are content with a gradual accumulation of minute
gains you will never be able to keep motivated and cheerful
enough to stay with a task.

I measure improvement in any one of three ways.

1 *Duration*. If your worrying currently lasts only half a day,
whereas formerly it habitually lasted all day, you are making
progress. To be sure, you are still neurotic, but you have cut
your neuroticism by half. Or if you now worry only two hours
and fifty-nine minutes whenever some crisis hits you (whereas
previously you worried three hours), you have made some
improvement. Do not look down your nose at this. It is a
genuine and valid change, and this is the stuff on which further
change is based. If you could reduce your worrying by one
minute a day, think what you could do with a three-hour
worrying problem in just 180 days. That is, in six months you
would have the entire problem beaten.

2 *Intensity*. Once you worried so much that you were ill,
couldn't sleep, and bit your nails. Now you worry so much less
that you get ill and bite your nails—but can sleep. Don't you
see that you have made improvement? Again you are certainly
neurotic, but you have stopped at least one of the symptoms.
That's improvement.

3 *Frequency*. If your tendency has been to worry twenty days
out of thirty and you are now worrying only nineteen days out
of thirty, you again have made some improvement, even though
you are still a confirmed worrier. If you could again reduce the
frequency by another day each week, in no time at all you
would have that problem beaten too.

Most people will simply not give themselves credit when they
have done a good job on their emotional disturbances. They do

not see that reducing the intensity, duration, or frequency of a symptom is an enormous step forward. But they deserve the credit and must be encouraged to see all of these changes as positive ones which, if they could be continued, would wipe out the emotional problem under consideration.

It is important for a person to stop thinking of improvement in all-or-nothing terms, which causes him to think he has not made improvement because he is still occasionally worried or fearful. If that were the case, none of us could claim improvement, because we are all occasionally worried or anxious or afraid. What we are trying to do is *reduce* the symptom in three ways if possible and to be content with any change in that direction.

I am convinced that the people who are successful in overcoming their personality difficulties are those who do not get discouraged because change is slow. They look for every little change and give themselves a pat on the back for what they have accomplished. They do not make godlike and unrealistic demands upon themselves. They know full well that the problem they are working on today may come back again— simply because they are human and because they cannot always be in full control. They are content with small steps and are able to add little gains upon little gains until they finally have substantial changes that everyone can notice. Do not minimize changes, regardless of how minute they might be. A mountain is a pile of tiny atoms, a beach is the accumulation of billions of grains of sand, and an ocean is a collection of billions of drops of rain. Learn to think in terms of little gains and gradual change and you will one day see big changes occurring in your life.

### Always work on self-esteem

If you do not think you are capable of overcoming your fear, you obviously cannot do so. However, in order to feel capable of doing anything you must have self-confidence and self-respect. You cannot have confidence if you do not respect yourself and have an image of yourself as a capable person. For this reason it is extremely important for anyone wishing to overcome the habit of worrying and being afraid that he cultivate within himself a feeling of self-esteem. Those who have self-esteem are willing to face any task. Those who do not have it can be slain by midgets. This is especially true when we see how readily people give in to fears that are practically inconsequential in the final analysis. Yet those persons with low self-confidence and low self-esteem almost invariably are overcome by the most ridiculous and simple tasks. One is afraid to enter the ring because he might be beaten. What harm could there be in being beaten? Another person is afraid to ask for a job because he might be turned down. What harm could there be in being rejected? Another is afraid to venture forth into a new field of work because he might do poorly in it. So what? How could this conceivably hurt him eternally? But in every such instance and millions more, you and I are thoughtlessly talking ourselves into thinking of these as horrible and catastrophic events over which we, insignificant and worthless people that we are, have no control. This is where one's low self-esteem shows itself most dramatically.

Then how does one overcome poor self-esteem? In two ways. The first is this: Never blame yourself for anything. Always separate your actions from yourself. Criticize your actions if you like, but never run yourself down because you have performed badly. Those who rate themselves by their actions are doomed to a life of misery and inferiority. The reason is simple. Since we are human, we will often behave badly. If we go around judging ourselves by that inevitable behaviour, we will end up believing that we are inferior.

The second important way to develop high self-esteem is this: Take a risk, stick your neck out, and do the thing you are afraid of. Then, after you have done less than perfectly, sit back objectively and look over your mistakes so that you can improve the next time. After all, progress is built on mistakes. The person who does not make mistakes does not learn.

66

Instead of being depressed and guilt-ridden because we have botched it, let us be content that we have discovered something. Making a mistake is an extremely important experience that tells us what *not* to do next time, rather than how worthless we are. It is not coincidental that even the greatest batsman can score a century in one innings and a duck in the next.

In both these ways you can develop self-esteem and self-confidence. Then by going through the experience you assure yourself that you are capable of it, and that you do not have to melt under the threat of something you are uncertain of. When I was in college I camped in the Rocky Mountains, and on one occasion it looked as if I might have to hike ten miles to town for help. The thought of going many miles through the woods caused me some apprehension until I realized that I had *already* walked twenty miles when I was in the Army. I was certain that walking ten miles through the Rockies could be no worse than the Army hike had been. This is how one gets self-confidence. You do the thing you are afraid to do and you prove to yourself over and over that you do not need to be afraid of experiences. The person with the most experience is the one who can compare the next experience to those that he has already had. Thus he can probably feel some assurance that what he is about to undertake is not a great deal worse than what he has already done.

If you feel that you are not as good as others, if you lower your eyes when you shake someone's hand, if you're always boasting about yourself as if to impress others, you have a low self-esteem and ought to get on the ball and do something about seeing yourself as more worthwhile. You do not have to be perfect in order to be worthwhile; you are worthwhile because you have life, and that is where your self-esteem comes from. Therefore, separate your *performance* from *yourself* just as you separate your ugly nose or your big toe from yourself as a human being. Even though it is an integral part of your body, there is nothing to prevent you from looking at your nose and saying that you dislike it without also disliking yourself as a person. Your nose, after all, is not your entire self, and neither is your occasional behaviour. Along with every stupid move you make, you also make a number of fine moves. You may have cheated the waiter on the bill this morning, but you also kindly opened the door for your friend, made a thoughtful telephone call to somebody, lent your coat to another person, and so on. Our poor behaviours are always sprinkled on a sea of fine and meritorious deeds. Let us therefore not colour ourselves evil because we occasionally perform badly. If you will see yourself as a fallible human being who is not a saint and who occasionally will do badly, you will find your self-esteem not being dragged down by your own self-loathing. Then you will see to it that the most important ingredient towards self-esteem and towards overcoming your emotional problems is taken care of.

# 7

# Putting It All Together

The following is a verbatim case study of a young, fearful male. The client is a college student who returned to school after being in the business world for several years. His first week back in the classroom was such a new experience for him that he became tense and feared he might pass out or be sick. This fear preyed on his thoughts so constantly he found it impossible to apply himself to his studies. To get control of himself before he might be forced to drop out of school he decided to receive psychotherapy.

*Client*  I came to see you because I have an ulcer and when I sit in class and get these fears and anxieties my stomach starts to churn in a knot and I get dizzy and lightheaded and feel I'm going to pass out and be sick. It's not just in school. It's in a lot of things I do. It's almost phobic. I can't ride in cars when other people are driving. I take stairs instead of elevators and things like this. Whenever I have to do something new, something strange (coming up here today produces it), I just get this horrible feeling almost like a paralyzing fear.

*Therapist*  How long have you had this?

*C*  Well, it's been coming on for about four years.

*T*  What other kind of fears do you have? Tell me all about those. Let's see how far this thing goes.

*C*  Let's see. Give me an instance if you can.

*T*  Height?

*C*  Yes.

*T*  Spiders?

*C*  No.

*T*  Crowds?

*C*  Yes, being hemmed in. Embarrassment, in front of people, in the classroom. I think I always felt sorry for the kids in school who were sick in class. Now I am terrified I am going to do it. Maybe I'll faint, although I never have.

T  Yes. How often have you seen someone faint or be sick?

C  Throw up—quite a few times. Faint—once, I believe, is all. I feel so sorry for them. Of course I've seen people in bars do it, but that isn't really so bad. It's mainly in school, in a crowd, in the middle of a street—I've seen that happen a few times. It sounds silly now. I see myself doing that and think how embarrassed I'd be and how everybody would turn against me and say, "Oh, look at that."

T  Let me tell you something about fear and how you get into that condition. Then you can think about this and we'll talk about it. The fear that you are experiencing is something which you are constantly giving yourself. You are a catastrophizer.

C  That sounds terrible.

T  Well, that's another catastrophizing statement right there.

C  Yes.

T  That's why you are in this predicament, because you make catastrophes out of everything—even the fact that I said you are a catastrophizer. You look out into this world you live in and correctly see certain things as potentially dangerous and harmful. For example, a crowded elevator might have a greater chance of falling than one that is not so crowded, because of that additional weight. So it's not exactly unrealistic to say: "I wonder if I shouldn't avoid crowded elevators, because the chances of something happening to them are increased over the ones that are empty." So far so good. However, when you say to yourself, "I should play it *perfectly* safe because anything is possible; and I must avoid crowded elevators at all costs; and it would be horrible if some of these things would happen," you're acting neurotically. For example, when you are saying: "If I ride in a car with someone else and *they're* driving, then I don't have any control over that car and I don't know what's going to happen. I trust my own driving, but I don't trust theirs as much as I do my own. Therefore, it really is true that I think I would be safer driving my own car rather than with someone else." But you make a catastrophe out of driving with someone else. You are saying: "What if I get injured? What if he doesn't drive as well as I do? What if he throws up? I might have a crash." Well, that's true. But then you're also saying: "That would be the *end of the world!*" And, "Shouldn't I think about that possibility all the time and *dwell upon it and make it a big mountain rather than a molehill?*" You build things way out of proportion until you have taken a grain of truth and you have made it an absolute certainty that it's going to kill you.

C    Forgive me for laughing, but when you say it that way it makes me feel—it sounds so silly—the whole thing.

T    Yes. But that's basically all it is, isn't it?

C    Yes.

T    It's your tendency to dwell upon a grain of truth and then to magnify it so out of proportion. For example, suppose I told you that you can die from getting a fish bone caught in your throat. Now that's true. And you could certainly develop a very nice fear of eating fish, because you would say, "What if I got a bone caught in my throat? I'd spit and sputter, and I'd throw up in the restaurant, and I could die for lack of air," and so on. Now you could just dwell on this from now until the next time you eat fish and you'd have one beautiful fear reaction, wouldn't you? Can you see how?

C    Yes, I would. Yes.

T    That is because you have taken a true statement, "People can die from eating fish," and you have now turned it into an absolute certainty by focusing upon it endlessly. Follow me?

C    Yes. But in the car, I think a lot of it has to do with my

71

being afraid of somebody else's driving. See, here we go again. If I were driving and if I were to throw up, I would be able to stop the car and get out. But if someone else were driving, I would have to explain what I was going to do or something like this.

T    Yes. I understand. Again, you're making a catastrophe over the possibility that you might not be able to stop the car in time, and you might not be able to explain to them and they might think you were a little bit weird. What's so catastrophic about that? Why is that the end of the world?

C    Because I would hate people to think I was making a fool of myself. When I was in grade school I was always fat, really fat, and the one they made fun of. And I always tried very, very hard not to do anything foolish, conspicuous, or anything like this. I wanted to be perfect, never to make a mistake, and thereby to stop their teasing. But anyway, I've got a long list of defeats. There are a lot of things I did do well, but I don't remember those. I dwell on the ones I did poorly.

T    That's the usual tendency you have, I'm afraid. And then you also said to yourself when you failed: "Failure is *horrible*. Failure *reflects upon me*. I'm no good if I fail. If I do something badly, *I'm a bad guy*." You equate your failing behaviour with you as a person, so that one means the other. Well, that is not true, but we can talk about that at another time. For the moment, notice again that all these things you did would not have disturbed you if you hadn't made a catastrophe out of them. You would not have been so scared if you hadn't dwelt upon them and made them big, big momentous things in your life and said: "O.K., so I failed. It's normal enough. I tried the best I could. I was inexperienced. So what's the big deal? I learned a lot."

C    But I failed.

T    I failed and that's *terrible* so I should dwell on possibly

72

failing again. You keep thinking that. Somebody might laugh at you, as though that could hurt. How can it hurt? You keep saying, "I don't want to be embarrassed." Well, then, don't be embarrassed. Nobody embarrasses you.

C   Well, it's hard to feel that way. If I threw up right now and you saw me, to me it would be crushing and just horrible.

T   Yes, because you would say to yourself: "This means I am not perfect. Look, I threw up in public and anybody who does that is not perfect and it's awful if you're not perfect." Well, now, since when? If I've got some hang-up about that and I go around thinking nobody should throw up in public, that's my neurotic hang-up. You don't have to go and judge yourself just because I'm disturbed. No, your embarrassment comes solely from you. If I threw up in front of you, I would say: "I'm sorry I did that. But if you're embarrassed by that, that's your problem. I'm not embarrassed. I just don't like throwing up. I refuse to compound my problem. I've got a problem with throwing up and I refuse to make it worse by becoming embarrassed also." Nobody embarrasses me but who? Me.

C   It sounds silly to hear you say what I feel. The fear is a real thing. It is sometimes paralyzing to me. At times when I have to face something I am really nervous about, I'll walk in circles, trying to decide to do it—fight or flight, do it or not, run away or stay. A lot of times I've run away.

T   That's no good. I would suggest for a beginning homework assignment to start doing some of the things you are afraid of and keep telling yourself, "I don't care all that much if I throw up. I don't care who likes it or not. I'm going to ride in elevators that are crowded, and I'll get off a floor earlier if I begin to get panicky. Also, I'm going to drive with somebody else, and if I get the

73

feeling that I'm going to throw up, I'm going to ask him to please stop the car. That's all."

C    But, see, I've never even thrown up. That's the thing.

T    You're probably not going to either. I practically guarantee that. That's just something up in your head. But unless you test your idea that it is really so horrible, that you can't face this, how are you going to learn that it is not that fearful? You keep saying things are fearful but you never test yourself. If I keep saying it's really not uncomfortable to go swimming in the ocean at six o'clock in the morning, and if you never test that statement, you'll never find out whether I'm right or not. You have to jump in, don't you. Right?

C    Right.

T    O.K. Let's do some of these things you are so afraid of and you'll find out whether or not all your assumptions are really true or false. You'll find out that they are a little bit true, but generally they will be largely false. However, you've got to keep doing it over and over to convince yourself of that.

C    I try to do some of them like riding in cars and things like this, but it depends a lot of time on the way my ulcer feels. Sometimes I can ride and it doesn't bother me too much, but a lot of times it's nervous anxiety, and then the fainting comes on, and then the ulcer starts to hurt, and then I get nauseous and the room starts spinning.

T    Again that's your catastrophizing. You are making too much of the whole thing, thinking about it all the time, and so on. There are some techniques that I want to teach you, ways to distract yourself, to learn to relax more and not to make such mountains out of molehills, and so on. They're fairly easily understood. You will have to work hard of course. If we talk about it often enough, I can teach you how you can overcome most of this anxiety and these fears that you are experiencing so that you can finally get rid of them.

[Notice how the first therapy session has achieved understanding of the client's problems and has already given him insight into how he is upsetting himself. He has his work cut out for him, but for the first time he knows what to do if he wants relief. He was given specific advice, his fears were treated as understandable psychological events, and he is now ready to practise what he has learned.

## *The next session*

*T*   What have you been doing? Let me hear.

*C*   Well, I've been riding in cars with people, three in the front seat (which I didn't like because I'm crowded), but I still had a little bit of phobia going the other night.

*T*   Where were you sitting?

*C*   I was driving.

*T*   Oh, you were driving.

*C*   Yes, which doesn't bother me too much. I haven't been brave enough to try riding with somebody else yet. But even with three in the front seat it's almost like a claustrophobia thing in that I get dizzy. Let's see, what else did I do? I've been riding in elevators, and I went to college every day. I've been trying to be a little more outgoing with people. Talked to them a little more. Struck up a little more conversation. That's about all I've been doing, it's tiring.

*T*   Yes, you're right. It's tiring because you really have to put forth effort. You have to face things. Facing things you are afraid of automatically tenses you up, doesn't it?

*C*   Yes, I know. This hasn't been my day so far. I was awful tense today.

*T*   Why are you tense today?

*C*   Well, I don't know. I wanted to ask you about this. Is there any way to fight a fear that is real? I have this fear that I'm not going to have enough money to finish college. Now is there some way you can get around that? Maybe it is exaggerated. Maybe I do have enough. As I

75

told you before, my dad did leave us some money and we went through that. Not that we squandered it, but we didn't do the best things with it. So now it's down. I shouldn't be insecure about that, but I am.

T    What you are saying is: "What if it isn't enough? Then shouldn't I worry about that?" No! Why should you worry about it? So you don't have enough. So you have to take off a year and work and save some. Maybe it takes you five years to get through school instead of four. Is that so serious?

C    I guess not.

T    Right. I would not like to see that but that wouldn't be the end of the world. How many guys in this community of half a million people do not have a college education and are providing for themselves and their families? A lot of them. I don't see any people dropping dead on the street, do you?

C    No.

T    Well, you're acting like that. What could happen to you? You'd still be able to earn a living.

C    Right. But I wouldn't be able to realize my ambitions, and that would be a tragic thing.

T    That would be a *sad* thing. It wouldn't be the end of the world. Who knows what you are already not fulfilling. If you had all your father's money and if your father had been alive, who knows where you might be today.

C    Right.

T    All right, so you're not there and that's not killing you. You don't even think about that now.

C    No. I suppose not.

T    All right, instead of worrying about it I would say, "Well, if I need more money, I'd better go to work."

C    Yes.

T    Do you have a job?

C    I have sort of an off-and-on job. I'm a salesman. My wife works. I have part ownership in a business. I know I am not going to starve to death. The whole idea is: I haven't got as much as I had before. So I wasted that money—or at least I think I did, whether I did or not—and so now I haven't got as much as I had before, and that scares me.

T    No. *It* doesn't scare you. *You* scare yourself by saying again: "This is *terrible*. This may indicate that I may not have enough money to finish my education, and that would be *unbearable*." Well, it *wouldn't* be unbearable. You just have to lump it, that's all.

C    [The client spoke about lending money too readily to his friends.]

T    Maybe that is why you are losing some of your own personal money—because you're an easy touch. That's another thing. Why can't you say no?

C    I don't know. I just don't want to hurt anyone's feelings.

T    But you don't hurt other people's feelings.

C    Here it goes—that same deal. I am afraid people won't like me. I want them to like me. I want them to keep liking me. So I am a pushover, I suppose.

T    So you give in so they will not reject you.

C    Yes.

T    Because ...

C    Because I want them to like me.

T    No. Not because you *want* them to like you. Because you think they *have* to like you and it would be *awful* if they didn't. You couldn't live if this guy rejected you.

C    Right.

T    That's the difference. Well now, why couldn't you live if he rejected you?

C    I suppose I could.

T    Do you really believe that?

C    Yes, I hate to think of losing a friend, though, because I lend money to my friends—which is probably dumb.

T    It's a good way to lose friends.

C    Right. So I say that's why I'd hate to lose one.

77

*T*  Have your feelings changed toward some of these good friends of yours to whom you've lent money?

*C*  Yes.

*T*  That's my point. See?

*C*  Yes. I wouldn't lend it again.

*T*  You've lost a little respect for them, haven't you? Because you know you have been taken advantage of. So the way to keep friendships, I usually think, is not to lend money to friends. Say, "Look, I am sorry. I don't have it." And let it go. He has probably been rejected by other friends. But if he is such a good friend, why would he reject you?

*C*  But is that really a fear? Isn't that more of an insecurity—the fear of not having the money; I mean, of running out of money?

*T*  A feeling of insecurity is a fear. You say, "Well, I feel insecure because I am afraid something is going to happen and I ought to be upset by that." I could say, "The world is going to end," but I don't need to feel insecure about it. The world will just have to end.

*C*  That's a hard concept to grasp—the fact that I don't care. I mean, what will happen will happen. It *shouldn't* bother me.

*T*  No, it *would be better* if I didn't bother you.

*C*  Right.

*T*  You can *let* it bother you if you want, as you might do in an airplane or a car. You came down here in your car today and you could have been killed.

*C*  Right.

*T*  But you weren't thinking about that possibility all the time, were you?

*C*  No. Lots of times before seeing you this anxiety thing made me feel that if I had been killed I wouldn't have cared. I think I would have been happier, you know, really. Because that anxiety just builds up until you think you are going to fly all to pieces.

78

*T*    Yes.

*C*    But, no, I don't think about getting killed. My wife is terribly touchy about that. We are driving along and she says, "Slow down! Watch this car! Watch that car!" The same thing happens in lightning and thunder storms. She wants to hide in the basement or something. And I don't think about it when driving, or anything like that.

*T*    All right, now analyze her fear for a moment, will you? What is she doing?

*C*    She's catastrophizing like you said I was—in elevators and things like that—taking a possible fear and blowing it all out of proportion.

*T*    Sure. Now you can see how she has her ways of making herself all nervous and fearful just as you did. You do it about different things.

*C*    I don't know if hers make her physically sick or not. I think they do. They make her edgy and moody and things like that. Especially in a storm. You can't stay in the same room with her. She paces around and looks out the window. I go out and stand in the rain, myself. I've tried talking to her about that too. I told her what you have said about catastrophizing and it helped her, I'm sure, because she has been better about it lately.

*T*    Good.

*C*    You make the whole thing look so ridiculous and silly. If people could do that at the time it would be fine. But it's just hard to make it look ridiculous and silly when you are in the middle of it.

*T*    To you it's an overwhelmingly dangerous and critical situation that must receive all kinds of attention.

*C*    It'll just take practice, I suppose, to get rid of it.

*T*    You have to challenge, you have to keep questioning these thoughts. It isn't the situations that are upsetting you, it's your thinking about them. A rainstorm doesn't bother you, but it disturbs your wife. Well, now, what's the difference? The rainstorm is going to affect her differently than you? She gets wet and you don't? In other words, she says certain neurotic thoughts to herself when there is a thunderstorm, and you don't say those things. Because she is saying neurotic things, she has a neurotic reaction. You don't say neurotic things, so you enjoy the storm, you don't have a neurotic reaction. When you begin to say neurotic things to yourself, *question* them. *Challenge* them, *debate* them, *throw them out*. Stop believing that they make sense and discard them. Then you could be broke and not nervous. You don't have to be nervous because you're in an elevator. You don't have to be nervous when you're driving three across the front seat of a car. You are simply making something out of that. Maybe your wife doesn't. Does she get nervous when you are three in a car?

C    No.

T    See what I mean? It just depends on what you want to focus on and disturb yourself over. It is one's thinking that does it. Every time you go after that thinking and beat it down, you are on the way to overcoming the fear.

C    Sometimes I don't even realize that I am thinking anything at all. I could be watching television and all of a sudden this anxiety comes up and that's strange, because I don't know what exactly to do in a case like that when I don't really know what's bothering me. Is it a symbolic thing when you see something on television?

T    It could be. Whether it is or not, however, you made something out of the television show. You alarmed yourself. You catastrophized about something you saw and weren't aware of doing so. Just tell yourself, "O.K., so unconsciously and unwittingly I catastrophized about something. So what? So I'm nervous now and I am going to be sweating beads of blood. That's too bad. However, I don't have to be upset because I'm nervous, do I?"

C    No.

T    This is usually what most people do. They make a

secondary worry or fear. They say, "I'm afraid of losing my job," and then they get all nervous. Later on it turns out that their job is O.K. and they don't have to worry about losing it, but then they worry about how awful it felt while they were worrying, and they wonder: "Am I ever going to feel like that again? It would be *terrible* if I had that nervousness come back." Then they begin to worry about that nervousness. It is not losing a job they are afraid of now. It is what?

C   It is the nervousness.

T   Yes.

C   What I have found is that the things I am afraid of are never as bad as what I perceive them to be beforehand. Like I think meeting somebody is going to be a certain way, and it is never quite that bad. Why do people build a think up like that?

T   Because that's the natural tendency when you start to catastrophize. You build things up bigger and bigger. You start out correctly saying: "Well, I don't know how I am going to get along with these people. I don't know if they are going to accept me. I don't know that I am going to look ignorant compared to them." O.K. Those are all true statements. You don't know that. Then you start to catastrophize by saying: "Well, wouldn't that be terrible? Wouldn't that be awful? Wouldn't I be humiliated? Shouldn't I worry about this possibility now? Shouldn't I think of all the possibilities that may come up so that I can have all the answers ready-made and won't get embarrassed?"

In other words, you begin to dread it. You begin to focus on it and to dwell upon it. Before you know it you are saying, "I'm going to meet the smartest man in the whole world; and I am the most ignorant man in the whole world; and this is going to be the most shameful experience in the whole world." Well, no wonder you're shaking like a leaf when you meet an ordinary man.

C    That's right. I suppose you could do that with just about any emotion, couldn't you? Jealousy or anything. Just blow it all out of proportion like that.

T    Yes. Absolutely, that's usually what jealousy is. It's a blowing out of proportion by thinking you have to have the other person's love. You say, "My wife looked at somebody and I am not sure that this doesn't mean that maybe she is interested in him. If it is possible that she might be interested in somebody else, I would find that *intolerable*. I would *have* to worry about that. It will *kill* me if she loves somebody else more than she loves me." And so on. That is nonsense. *Why* would it kill you? If she doesn't love you, marry somebody else.

C    I'm not jealous, I don't have that problem. But I was just thinking. ... I suppose I am a little jealous. I suppose everybody is, aren't they, to a certain extent?

T    It is an easy thing to do. Most people are.

C    Now how do you go about fighting this sort of a phobic thing? The same way you do as with a fear, just face it and say, "Why do I feel this way?"

T    What phobia are you talking about?

C    Fear of confinement and things like that.

T    That is not a phobia.

C    That's not? Claustrophobia?

T    Claustrophobia is a phobia. They define it that way. But in your case, you know what you are afraid of. In other words, this business of being confined means, "I am afraid that if I get too confined, I won't be able to get out when I get nervous."

C    Right.

T    So you *know* what you are afraid of. Now with a phobia, the fear is something which you *think* you're afraid of but you aren't afraid of that at all. For example, a claustrophobia, as I see it and define the term (and I don't know if everybody agrees with me on this) is a symbolic

82

fear, not just an unusual or unreasonable fear. You'd have to be thinking you were afraid of being hemmed in, when really the thing you were afraid of is being smothered by your mother, for example.

C   Oh, I see.

T   But you can't admit that. Instead you say to yourself, "My mother is very possessive, and like a spider she hovers over me. She has a hundred legs and arms and just won't let me move." You might not be able to admit that because you might feel very guilty about saying: "I have a mother whom I want to reject. I want to push her back and tell her to leave me alone. But that would make me feel very guilty." So instead of that you say, "I can't stand closed-in places."

C   Do you almost have to develop a coldhearted outlook towards people and reality?

T   Absolutely. I think it is very healthy to look at things objectively and with little sentimentality. I find most neurotics are terribly sensitive people. They are so sensitive that whatever happens in their lives makes them go bananas instead of being somewhat hard and thick-skinned about it. It is very important, if you want to be a healthy person, to be thick-skinned.

Okay. Our time is about up. Let me wind up by complimenting you on what a nice job you've done. Your symptoms have lessened considerably since our first session. If you continue at this pace, we shouldn't be needing more than a few sessions.

Gee, I'm glad to hear you say that. I also thought I was doing fine, but I was afraid to pat myself on the back for fear I might be fooling myself.

T   True, I often find my clients not giving themselves enough credit for the splendid work they've done. They wouldn't hesitate to reprimand themselves if their symptoms took a turn for the worse. But giving themselves a reward seems like self-indulgence.

C   It sure does. Is it really so important to reward myself when I've done well? After all, isn't the improvement itself reward enough?

T   Not always. I want you to reward yourself with a pleasant thought each time you manage a fear better than you did before. Actually tell yourself that you did a good job. Tell yourself how beautifully self-disciplined you were, how you're gaining increasing mastery over your neurotic emotions and even doing better than other people whom you've often envied. That's how I want you to praise your progress, not yourself, in an open and completely unashamed way.

C   How did you mean that? I should praise my progress, not myself?

T   Yes. Don't think you're some sort of superhuman being merely because you are getting better at a skill. If you do that, you'll feel like you're worthless and inferior when you begin to lose that skill or someone outshines you. Don't judge yourself by your behaviour, ever. You as a human being and your actions are not the same. Separate them always and you'll never get depressed from self-blame. If you do the same thing for other people, you'll never get angry. Either way you stand to gain.

C   You mean that when I do well I am still me and not somebody I wasn't before. I've just learned something new perhaps, and that doesn't have to give me a big head.

T   Of course. Would you suggest for instance that anyone who is afraid as you were a few weeks ago is just no good as a human being?

C   No, certainly not. By the same token I wasn't worthless before I learned to conquer my worries and I'm not more worthwhile now that I'm beginning to conquer them.

T   That's it. I find it to be a particularly difficult idea to accept: that we need never judge ourselves by our actions. If you're like everyone else, you'll continue to do this for quite some time yet.

84

## Summary

In two more sessions the client gained enough control over his worrying and fear so that we could safely terminate psychotherapy. He was one of those fortunate persons who could understand what I was saying and then work hard to put my advice into practice. Other people have a tougher time of it: they don't grasp the philosophy of calmness—they continue to insist that things must disturb them and that they have little control over their feelings unless their life problems vanish. I hope these two abridged transcripts have shown that nothing needs to change in your life and that you can still learn to calm down about situations you once believed made you tense.

The client's life situation did not change significantly. He still attended college. He was still in danger of doing something for which he could be criticized or laughed at. He still had the same financial problems. Yet he changed his thinking *about* these situations and *that* is what finally gave him peace of mind.

He could also have got over his worries if I had magically been able to remove his problems. And if I could have done so, I would have. I would have urged him to change his frustrations all he humanly could. In the event, however, that he could not change them completely or enough to suit him, he would have been left with the burden of living calmly with them.

This, and *nothing* else, in the final analysis, is the insight you had better accept if you want emotional peace. Nothing short of your talking yourself out of *overconcern* is going to do the trick in connection with those frustrations which you cannot remove. The client saw this fact clearly, so he applied himself to the practical task of changing his thinking, whether he liked the idea or not.

I urge you also to accept reality and finally to understand that life is full of danger, heartache, and injustice, but that if you focus on them unduly, you will create more danger, more heartache, and more injustice—to others and to yourself. And that's what this book is all about. If you want a saner, calmer world, start with yourself as your first project. When you have yourself reasonably under control, go forth and apply these principles to others.

# Overcoming Common Problems

## MAIL ORDER FORM

**THE ABC OF EATING** *Joy Melville*                                       cased £6.95 ☐
Coping with anorexia, bulimia and compulsive eating                        paper £2.50 ☐

**AN A–Z OF ALTERNATIVE MEDICINE**                                         cased £6.95 ☐
*Brent Hafen and Kathryn Fraudsen*                                         paper £2.50 ☐

**ARTHRITIS** *Dr William Fox*
Is your suffering really necessary?                                         paper £2.50 ☐

**BIRTH OVER THIRTY** *Sheila Kitzinger*                                    cased £6.95 ☐
                                                                           paper £2.50 ☐

**BODY LANGUAGE** *Allan Pease*                                             cased £7.95 ☐
                                                                           paper £2.95 ☐

**CALM DOWN** *Dr Paul Hauck*
How to cope with frustration and anger                                     paper £2.50 ☐

**DEPRESSION** *Dr Paul Hauck*                                             cased £6.95 ☐
                                                                           paper £2.50 ☐

**DIVORCE AND SEPARATION** *Angela Willans*                                cased £6.95 ☐
Everywoman's guide to a new life                                           paper £2.50 ☐

**ENJOYING MOTHERHOOD** *Dr Brice Pitt*
How to have a happy pregnancy                                              paper £2.50 ☐

**THE EPILEPSY HANDBOOK** *Shelagh McGovern*                               paper £3.95 ☐

**FAMILY FIRST AID** *Dr Andrew Stanway*                                   paper £3.95 ☐

**FEARS AND PHOBIAS** *Dr Tony Whitehead*                                  paper £2.50 ☐

**FEELING HEALTHY** *Dr F E Kenyon*                                        paper £2.50 ☐

**FIT KIT** *David Lewis*                                                         £2.99 ☐

**FLYING WITHOUT FEAR** *Tessa Duckworth and David Miller*                 cased £6.95 ☐
                                                                           paper £2.50 ☐

**GOODBYE BACKACHE** *Dr David Imrie with Colleen Dimson*                  cased £7.95 ☐
An easy, practical way to a pain-free and healthy back                     paper £3.95 ☐

**GUILT** *Dr Vernon Coleman*
Why it happens and how to overcome it                                      paper £2.50 ☐

**THE HEARTACHE OF MOTHERHOOD** *Joyce Nicholson*                          paper £2.95 ☐

**HERPES** *Dr Oscar Gillespie*
What to do when you have it                                                paper £3.95 ☐

**HOW TO BRING UP YOUR CHILD SUCCESSFULLY** *Dr Paul Hauck*                paper £2.95 ☐

**HOW TO CONTROL YOUR DRINKING** *Dr W Miller and Dr R Munoz*             paper £3.95 ☐

**HOW TO COPE WITH STRESS** *Dr Peter Tyrer*                               paper £2.50 ☐

**HOW TO COPE WITH YOUR NERVES** *Dr Tony Lake*                            cased £6.95 ☐
                                                                           paper £2.50 ☐

**HOW TO DO WHAT YOU WANT TO DO** *Dr Paul Hauck*                          paper £2.50 ☐

**HOW TO LOVE AND BE LOVED** *Dr Paul Hauck*                               cased £6.95 ☐
                                                                           paper £2.50 ☐

**HOW TO SLEEP BETTER** *Dr Peter Tyrer*                                   paper £2.50 ☐

**HOW TO STAND UP FOR YOURSELF** *Dr Paul Hauck*                           paper £2.50 ☐

**JEALOUSY** *Dr Paul Hauck*                                    cased £5.95 ☐
Why it happens and how to overcome it                           paper £2.50 ☐
**LONELINESS** *Dr Tony Lake*                                   paper £2.50 ☐
**MAKING MARRIAGE WORK** *Dr Paul Hauck*                        paper £2.50 ☐
**MAKING THE MOST OF MIDDLE AGE** *Dr Brice Pitt*               paper £2.50 ☐
**MEETING PEOPLE IS FUN** *Dr Phyllis Shaw*
How to overcome shyness                                         paper £2.50 ☐
**NO MORE HEADACHES** *Lilian Rowen*                            paper £99p ☐
**ONE PARENT FAMILIES** *Diana Davenport*                       paper £2.50 ☐
**OVERCOMING TENSION** *Dr Kenneth Hambly*                      paper £2.50 ☐
**SELF-HELP FOR YOUR ARTHRITIS** *Edna Pemble*                  paper £2.50 ☐
**THE SEX ATLAS** *Erwin Haeberle*                              paper £10.00 ☐
**SIX WEEKS TO A HEALTHY BACK** *Alexander Melleby*             cased £6.95 ☐
                                                                paper £2.50 ☐
**SOLVING YOUR PERSONAL PROBLEMS** *Peter Honey*               cased £6.95 ☐
                                                                paper £2.50 ☐
**STRESS AND YOUR STOMACH** *Dr Vernon Coleman*                 paper £2.50 ☐
**SUCCESSFUL SEX** *Dr F E Kenyon*                              paper £2.50 ☐
**WHAT EVERYONE SHOULD KNOW ABOUT DRUGS** *Kenneth Leech*       cased £6.50 ☐
                                                                paper £2.50 ☐
**WHY BE AFRAID?** *Dr Paul Hauck*                              paper £2.50 ☐

All these books can be ordered direct by post. Just tick the titles you want and fill in the form below.

Name ..............................................................................................................

Address ..............................................................................................................

..............................................................................................................

..............................................................................................................

Write to OCP Mail Order, SPCK, Marylebone Road, London NW1 4DU. Please enclose remittance to the value of the cover price plus:
UK: 50p for the first book plus 32p per copy for each additional book ordered.
Overseas: 75p for the first book plus 45p per copy for each additional book.

Sheldon Press reserve the right to show new retail prices on covers which may differ from those previously advertised in the text or elsewhere. Postage rates are also subject to revision.